I0426119

# Protocol for Monitoring Fish Communities in Small Streams in the Heartland Inventory and Monitoring Network

Natural Resource Report NPS/HTLN/NRR—2008/052

Hope R. Dodd, David G. Peitz, Gareth A. Rowell, David E. Bowles, and Lloyd W. Morrison

National Park Service
Heartland I&M Network
Wilson's Creek National Battlefield
6424 West Farm Road 182
Republic, Missouri 65738

August 2008

U.S. Department of the Interior
National Park Service
Natural Resource Program Center
Fort Collins, Colorado

The Natural Resource Publication series addresses natural resource topics that are of interest and applicability to a broad readership in the National Park Service and to others in the management of natural resources, including the scientific community, the public, and the NPS conservation and environmental constituencies. Manuscripts are peer-reviewed to ensure that the information is scientifically credible, technically accurate, appropriately written for the intended audience, and is designed and published in a professional manner.

Natural Resource Reports are the designated medium for disseminating high priority, current natural resource management information with managerial application. The series targets a general, diverse audience, and may contain NPS policy considerations or address sensitive issues of management applicability. Examples of the diverse array of reports published in this series include vital signs monitoring plans; monitoring protocols; "how to" resource management papers; proceedings of resource management workshops or conferences; annual reports of resource programs or divisions of the Natural Resource Program Center; resource action plans; fact sheets; and regularly-published newsletters.

Views, statements, findings, conclusions, recommendations and data in this report are solely those of the author(s) and do not necessarily reflect views and policies of the U.S. Department of the Interior, NPS. Mention of trade names or commercial products does not constitute endorsement or recommendation for use by the National Park Service.

Printed copies of reports in these series may be produced in a limited quantity and they are only available as long as the supply lasts. This report is also available from the Natural Resource Publications Management website (http://www.nature.nps.gov/publications/NRPM) and the Heartland Inventory and Monitoring website (http://science.nature.nps.gov/im/units/htln) on the Internet or by sending a request to the address on the back cover.

Please cite this publication as:

Dodd, H.R. , D. G. Peitz, G. A. Rowell, D. E. Bowles, and L. M. Morrison. 2008. Protocol for monitoring fish communities in small streams in the Heartland Inventory and Monitoring Network. Natural Resource Report NPS/HTLN/NRR—2008/052. National Park Service, Fort Collins, Colorado.

NPS D-79, August 2008

# Contents

# Figures

# Tables

# I. Background and Objectives

## Issues Being Addressed and Rationale for Fish Community Monitoring

Many lotic systems in the United States are in a degraded condition, largely as a result of watershed level land use changes and corresponding water pollution problems (USEPA, 1990). During the last century, large portions of grassland landscapes have been converted to cropland or livestock pasture (Knopf and Samson, 1997) increasing sedimentation, nutrient loading, and other chemical pollution in streams. Nonpoint source pollution from agricultural practices is regarded as the largest long-term threat to streams in the Midwest (USEPA, 1995). Other activities such as logging and urban development also negatively impact water quality by increasing surface water runoff and introducing chemical pollutants and soil from upland areas. These land use changes and resulting water quality alterations modify the natural hydrology and physical habitat of streams, and are exacerbated by flood events. Impacts to stream integrity and habitat include increase in spate intensity, shifts in channel geomorphology and increased bed and bank erosion, altered light penetration and water temperature regimes. Although protecting riparian corridors may help mitigate some of these problems (Peterjohn and Correll, 1984; Osborne and Kovacic, 1993; Stauffer *et al.*, 2000), changes in land use practices within the watershed can overwhelm localized protection of stream corridors (Richards *et al.*, 1996; Roth *et al.*, 1996; Wang *et al.*, 1997; Weigel *et al.*, 2000). Because processes occurring in the entire watershed and the riparian areas are not independent of each other (Doppelt *et al.*, 1993), improving or maintaining stream integrity through partial protection of the watershed or stream corridor can be difficult and, in certain situations, impractical.

The National Park Service (NPS) has mandated that park managers establish baseline data or "vital signs" and long-term monitoring programs for the natural resources found within their parks. Monitoring information is intended to help address current resource problems while allowing managers to anticipate and plan for future resource issues. Maintaining the integrity of stream ecosystems so that they remain comparable to unimpaired streams of the region clearly warrants monitoring (Karr and Dudley, 1981; Angermeier and Karr, 1994). Because small streams in the Heartland Inventory and Monitoring Network (HTLN) have a relatively small area of their watersheds located within park boundaries, these streams are at risk of degradation due to adjacent land use practices and other anthropogenic disturbances. To monitor the status of aquatic resources, one or more biotic components (e.g., aquatic vegetation, invertebrates, fish) of a stream may serve to measure its ecological integrity. Fish communities of lotic systems are an important component of their aquatic ecosystems. Many fish species are considered intolerant of habitat alterations (Karr, 1981; Robison and Buchanan, 1988; Pflieger, 1997; Barbour *et al.*, 1999) and monitoring their assemblages can serve as a useful tool to assess changes in water and habitat quality (Hoefs and Boyle, 1990; Peitz, 2005; Petersen and Justus, 2005a, 2005b, 2005c, 2005d). Accordingly, trends in the composition and abundance of fish populations historically have been used to assess the biological integrity of streams (Barbour *et al.*, 1999; Moulton *et al.*, 2002). Moreover, the intrinsic value of fish to the public as environmental indicators and as a recreational opportunity makes the status of fish diversity a valuable interpretive topic for park visitors and an informative tool for supporting management decisions.

Many native fish populations have been impacted adversely throughout their ranges by a number of factors associated with land use changes and the loss of natural habitat. Among these impacts are habitat loss due to stream degradation and modification such as channel dewatering, impoundments, channelization and fragmentation, in-stream gravel mining, and siltation. Biological impacts stemming from the introduction of non-native fishes also have influenced the decline of native species (Kolar and Lodge, 2002). As a result of habitat loss and decline of water quality conditions in Midwestern streams, the Topeka shiner (*Notropis topeka*), a native prairie stream fish, has been listed as federally endangered under the Endangered Species Act of 1973. Currently, the Topeka shiner inhabits less than 10% of its historic range (Tabor, 1998). Similarly, the Arkansas darter (*Etheostoma cragini*) is a candidate for listing as threatened. This species is now found only in tributaries of the Arkansas River (Pflieger, 1997). In addition to these federally protected species, several other stream fishes are impaired due to habitat loss and fragmentation in the Midwest, making it necessary for state agencies to protect these native species within their jurisdictions (see Table 2 in SOP 9). Although anthropogenic disturbances at the watershed scale can dramatically alter a lotic system, protecting portions of small streams on publicly owned lands may offer refuges for these species as well as other native species. NPS lands provide some of the least impacted stream habitat remaining in the Midwest. As such, waterways on some NPS lands may contain habitat critical for sustaining populations of native fishes (Federal Register, 2002).

Because changes or shifts in stream habitat complexity and water quality often determine biotic communities, including fish (Lazorchak et al., 1998), monitoring trends in fish community composition along with associated habitat conditions serves as a strong basis for measuring stream integrity. Assessment of chemical/physical characteristics in lotic systems is a common practice used to monitor aquatic conditions and determine potential areas of degradation or resource problems. This type of water quality assessment gives investigators immediate results, but requires that sampling occur during or soon after a disturbance. Monitoring of biological resources complements water quality assessments because it can be used to assess longer term effects of disturbances on the aquatic system. A comprehensive monitoring program should include biotic indicators that respond or are linked to the physical and chemical conditions within the system. Information obtained from monitoring trends in fish communities, together with chemical and physical data, provides an integrated and robust assessment of stream integrity. Therefore, monitoring the current status and population trends of fish communities and their habitats is an important tool for preserving and conserving aquatic resources in the national parks.

The framework for monitoring small streams located in HTLN parks is directed towards maintaining their ecological integrity, which will be assessed through periodic monitoring of fish communities, physical habitat, and water quality. This protocol has been designed to incorporate the spatial relationship of biotic indicators with chemical constituents and physical habitat.

## History of Monitoring Fish Communities in Small Streams

In 2001-2003, the Prairie Cluster Prototype Long-term Ecological Monitoring Program began developing a protocol and initiated fish sampling at Pipestone National Monument (PIPE) and Tallgrass Prairie National Preserve (TAPR) to assess the integrity of prairie streams within their boundaries. Because the NPS was interested in locating and monitoring populations of the federally endangered Topeka shiner, the primary emphasis of this initial work was determining the status of this species, with secondary objectives of describing baseline fish communities and refining sampling techniques for prairie streams. A monitoring protocol for fish communities in prairie streams was developed for these two parks (hereafter called "prairie fish protocol", see Peitz and Rowell, 2004) and subsequent sampling was completed in 2004 and 2005. Fish communities and stream habitat were sampled at Homestead National Monument (HOME) in 2003 and 2004 (Peitz, 2005) using methods described in the prairie fish protocol (Peitz and Rowell, 2004). The primary purpose of this survey was to locate Topeka shiners and available habitat for this species within the park. In 2006, monitoring was continued at HOME using revised methods described in this protocol.

Aquatic monitoring in the smaller streams of HTLN historically has been limited to a handful of prairie parks and focused primarily on the aquatic invertebrate community or water quality. Other than the long term monitoring of Topeka shiner populations at PIPE and TAPR, fish communities in smaller parks of HTLN have been surveyed only sporadically and primarily for the purpose of developing faunal inventories: George Washington Carver National Monument (GWCA) (Petersen and Justus, 2005c), Hot Springs National Park (HOSP) (Petersen and Justus, 2005a), Pea Ridge National Military Park (PERI) (Petersen and Justus, 2005d), and Wilson's Creek National Battlefield (WICR) (Donegon, 1984; Foster, 1988; Hoeffs and Boyle, 1990; Petersen and Justus, 2005b). Pilot fish monitoring was initiated at GWCA, and WICR in 2006 to provide a more complete picture of the aquatic resources in these small streams. Several other network parks have notable aquatic resources, although long-term fish monitoring has not been conducted in those parks. These parks include Herbert Hoover National Historic Site (HEHO), Effigy Mounds National Monument (EFMO), HOSP, and PERI. Managers in these parks have limited or no information about the status of their aquatic resources. This protocol addresses this informational deficiency and describes methods for collecting fish community and habitat data (in-stream, riparian), in addition to diel CORE5 water quality data, in the previously listed parks. In total, this protocol describes monitoring of fish communities and their habitats in nine HTLN parks (EFMO, GWCA, HEHO, HOME, HOSP, PERI, PIPE, TAPR, WICR).

## Revision of Historic Protocol

The original prairie fish protocol (Peitz and Rowell, 2004) focused on the Topeka shiner and its primary habitat (pools). While monitoring the status of the Topeka shiner is important, it is difficult to effectively monitor this species without extensive sampling effort. To document its status with confidence, it would be necessary to sample several times a year, particularly during breeding season when individuals are concentrated, and to track population dynamics with mark/recapture techniques. The sampling period for PIPE and TAPR (late August through October) was established to avoid the breeding season so the additional stress of sampling would not cause mortality among this already rare species. In an internal NPS memo (Gary Williams, January 2002) summarizing the results of the prototype operation review, it was recommended that fish monitoring should be focused on the entire community and not a single species. Therefore, the underlying objectives and sampling methods in this revised protocol are re-focused toward the collection of data for the entire fish community. To accomplish these objectives, a reach-based approach similar to that used in other national-level protocols will be employed. Information on relative abundance of Topeka shiner will continue to be collected under this protocol allowing comparison with historic data collected under the original protocol. In addition, important information will be collected on the entire fish community (richness, diversity, abundance, size structure, and composition), which interacts with and influences Topeka shiner populations.

Several key modifications to Peitz and Rowell (2004) are described in this protocol that incorporate current scientific thinking. A summary of these changes can be found in Table 1. In general, the proposed changes will increase sample efficiency and enhance data quality and quantity without compromising the use of historic data in analyses of newly collected data. Details of modifications to the original prairie fish protocol are given below:

- Objectives are re-focused to include monitoring the entire fish community rather than an individual species. Therefore, all available habitats and channel units within a reach will be sampled.

- This protocol is expanded to include fish community monitoring in small streams at nine parks: EFMO, GWCA, HEHO, HOME, HOSP, PERI, PIPE, TAPR, and WICR.

- Historically, multiple reaches were sampled on streams at PIPE, TAPR, and HOME. In this protocol, only one representative reach per stream will be sampled at all nine parks. However, two historic sites on Pipestone Creek at PIPE and two sites on stream #1 at TAPR are retained because of a continued interest in monitoring Topeka shiner populations at those parks (see Sampling Design section below).

- Under this protocol, PIPE and TAPR will continue to be sampled annually, but the remaining seven parks will be sampled on a three year rotation (see Sampling Design section below).

- Seining will continue to be the only means for sampling fish at PIPE, TAPR, and HOME. This approach is retained because seining is the most efficient method for the sandy bottom and turbid water of Cub Creek (HOME), and it reduces stress on

Topeka shiners at PIPE and TAPR. Retaining this approach will also allow comparisons with historical data collected under the original protocol.

- Fish collection methods for EFMO, GWCA, HEHO, HOSP, PERI, and WICR follow Petersen *et al.* (2008), which is based on the existing US Geological Survey National Water-Quality Assessment (USGS NAWQA) fish protocol (Moulton *et al.*, 2002). The broad diversity of substrate composition and habitat conditions of streams in these parks require use of an electrofishing method.

- Under the previous protocol, only Topeka shiners were measured and weighed while all other species were counted. Under this protocol, length and weight will be measured for a subsample of up to 30 individuals of each species at each sample reach.

Table 1. Revisions and additions made to the original fish protocol (Peitz and Rowell, 2004).

| Change Made | Original Protocol | Revised Protocol |
|---|---|---|
| Objectives of monitoring | Topeka Shiner status | Fish Community |
| Channel units sampled | Pools | All available habitat |
| Number of parks | 2 | 9 |
| Sampling reaches | Multiple per stream | 1 per stream[1] |
| Sampling frequency | Annually | Annually for PIPE and TAPR; 3 year rotation for other parks |
| Sampling gear | Seine | Seine at PIPE, TAPR, HOME Electrofishing at other parks |
| Fish community data | Topeka shiners measured; all other fish counted | A 30 specimen subsample of each species measured; remaining fish counted |
| In-stream habitat assessment | Single reading taken at middle of each pool sampled | Taken at 3 transects in each channel unit at PIPE, TAPR, HOME ; 11 transects among entire reach at other parks |
| Velocity | Not collected | Collected at transects with flow meter and wading rod |
| Water quality | Static CORE 5 readings (hand-held meters) | Unattended hourly CORE 5 readings (datasonde) |
| | | [1] Two historic reaches retained at PIPE and Stream 1 at TAPR |

- Previously, in-stream habitat data were collected only at a single data point in pools where fish were seined. At PIPE, TAPR, and HOME where seining methods are used, habitat will be assessed at three transects within each channel unit (riffle, run, pool) sampled with one data point per transect (*i.e.*, three data points per channel unit sampled). At the remaining parks where electrofishing methods are employed, an 11 transect method will be used within the entire reach (after Petersen et al., 2008). Additionally, current velocity will be measured at each transect at each park. See SOP #5 for details on habitat assessments.

- In lieu of static CORE5 water quality measurements that were collected historically at PIPE, TAPR, and HOME using hand–held meters, hourly water quality measurements will be collected at each sample reach within each park using datasonde loggers. The one exception is TAPR, where static readings will continue to be collected due to the large number of reaches and few number of data loggers available. See SOP #3 for details.

- One disadvantage of implementing this revised protocol is that by sampling only once every three years instead of annually, it will potentially take longer to detect changes or significant trends in stream condition.

## Monitoring Objectives Addressed by the Protocol

Two broad objectives are addressed by this protocol: 1) Determine the status and long term trends in fish richness, diversity, abundance, and community composition in small streams at EFMO, GWCA, HEHO, HOME, HOSP, PERI, PIPE, TAPR, WICR, and 2) Correlate the long-term community data to overall water quality and habitat condition (DeBacker *et al.*, 2005).

## Justification/Rationale for these Objectives

The fish communities and their corresponding physical habitats and water quality have not been consistently inventoried or monitored in seven of the nine parks included in this protocol. With the exception of TAPR, the watersheds of these small streams remain largely unprotected, leaving them at risk to anthropogenic disturbance. Through long-term monitoring of these vulnerable aquatic resources, natural variability in fish communities, habitat and water quality can be quantified such that trends or changes in these aquatic components can be used to support management decisions in the parks. The initial years of data collection along with available historical data from within the park or watershed will provide an estimate of natural variability among these populations and establish baseline conditions for the assessment of temporal changes and maintenance of stream integrity. Measuring water quality, habitat structure and availability, and watershed land use patterns and correlating these with fish community composition will allow insight into the relative influences these variables have on the integrity of these small stream ecosystems.

# II. Sampling Design

## Spatial Design

This protocol focuses on monitoring fish communities in wadeable streams distributed among nine HTLN parks. Sampling will be conducted at a single reach for each stream. Greater sampling effort per stream is not possible due to limited budgets and resources in relationship to the relatively large number of target streams and parks sampled. Furthermore, most of the streams included in this protocol are relatively small, and the lengths of stream within the park boundaries are relatively short. An additional benefit of this approach is that it allows for monitoring fish communities in a greater number of network parks.

## Sample Reaches

A sample reach is a section of stream that encompasses all channel units (riffles, runs, pools, glides) available within the stream, resulting in a representative fish sample. Some streams sampled under this protocol are characterized primarily by one or two channel unit types (pools and runs); and, therefore, only those channel units will be represented in the sample reach. For each stream, the sample reach will be established at the downstream end of the watershed. The rationale for this choice is that the further one goes downstream, the more representative the site is of the overall watershed. If reaches were selected randomly, sites could be located near the upstream park boundary, in which case they may be more representative of the stream and associated watershed above the park than within the park.

The location of the reach will be near the downstream park boundary for streams that flow outside of the park or, for tributary streams that intersect larger streams within the park, near the confluence (but out of the floodplain) of the larger stream. The exact location of each reach will be based on availability of water for sampling, safety of personnel, accessibility, and ability to co-locate sites for other vital signs monitoring (*i.e.*, aquatic invertebrates). Locating reaches based on the ability to sample effectively and safely is consistent with other national-level guidance (Moulton *et al.*, 2002).

Historically Sampled Parks:

At PIPE, TAPR and HOME, reaches were established during fish sampling conducted under the prairie fish protocol (Peitz and Rowell, 2004). To retain comparability with historic data, we will use a subset of these established reaches. Location of these reaches and reach length was based on the ability to find areas of the stream with adequate water to collect fish from five pools. Reaches that were included in the original protocol that have since been observed to be consistently dry are removed from further consideration in this protocol, and the most downstream reach on each stream will be retained for sampling (Table 2). In addition, one historical reach at both PIPE and TAPR that is not located at the downstream end of the watershed will be retained: (1) The upper most reach located above the falls at PIPE will be retained due to differences in water quality and habitat composition compared to reaches below the falls. Retaining this second reach at PIPE may provide insight into environmental conditions of the stream as it enters the park and the effect these conditions may have on the downstream fish community. (2)

Reach 1 Middle at TAPR will be retained because this site has consistently produced Topeka shiners. Although this protocol focuses on fish communities, it remains important that the status of Topeka shiners be monitored for reporting purposes to the parks and the US Fish & Wildlife Service. A reach on Fox Creek at TAPR was added due to the lack of information on fish communities in this stream. Within each reach, three to five sites or channel units (riffle, run, pool, glide) will be seined for fish and corresponding habitat data collected. Site locations will be based on the availability of channel units within the reach at the time of sampling. See Peitz and Rowell (2004) for GPS coordinates of historical sites not included in this protocol. Maps displaying the original sites and those retained for sampling are in Appendix A.

Additional Parks:

Sampling reaches for streams within EFMO, GWCA, HEHO, HOSP, PERI, and WICR will be established to satisfy specific requirements necessary to obtain a representative and unbiased sample. The downstream end of the reach is determined *a priori* and located as close to the downstream park boundary as possible or located just upstream of the floodplain for tributaries that flow into larger streams within the park. Reach length is defined as 20 times the mean wetted stream width (MWSW), allowing inclusion of representative channel units (riffle, run, and pool habitats) located within the stream (Moulton *et al.*, 2002). Once established, this reach will become a permanent sampling site barring dramatic alterations in channel morphology that would require relocation of the sampling reach. Because GWCA and WICR also have long-term invertebrate monitoring, fish reaches will be co-located with the downstream most historical invertebrate sites in these parks. See Table 3 for a list of streams sampled at these parks. Maps of sampled streams are located in Appendix A.

*GWCA:*

Carver Creek. The lower reach boundary is about 15 m downstream of the west visitor's trail crossing Carver Creek.

Harkins Branch. The lower reach boundary is located immediately upstream of the downstream (west) park boundary fence.

Williams Branch. The lower boundary is about 130 m downstream of the west visitor's trail crossing Williams Branch.

*WICR:*

Skegg's Branch. The lower boundary is about 30 m upstream from the tour road.

Wilson's Creek. The lower boundary begins at old bridge crossing of Old Wire Road.

Terrell Creek.  A reach was established during pilot sampling at WICR in 2006. The lower boundary is approximately 70 m upstream of Highway ZZ bridge.

Table 2. List of stream reaches retained for sampling in this protocol along with UTM coordinates (NAD83 (Conus), Zone 14 N) and justification for including each reach. Those reaches shaded in gray will no longer be monitored because they are often dry during the sampling period.

| Stream Reaches Previously Sampled | Reaches to be Retained | UTM (Northing, Easting) | Justification |
|---|---|---|---|
| **PIPE** | | | |
| Pipestone Creek Lower<br>Pipestone Creek Middle<br>Pipestone Creek Upper | Lower | 4877259.61, 714204.77 | Lower reach: most downstream site; effective with seine; high numbers of Topeka shiners |
| Pipestone Creek Above Falls | Above Falls | 4877060.11, 714772.31 | Above reach: separated by falls - major differences in habitat and water quality from the 3 sites below the falls |
| **TAPR** | | | |
| 01 Lower<br>01 Middle<br>01 Upper | Lower<br>Middle* | 4257009.20, 713468.40<br>4257264.29, 713122.37 | Lower reach: most downstream site<br>*Middle reach: consistent and high numbers of Topeka shiners |
| 02 Lower<br>02 Middle | Lower | 4256214.78, 713417.68 | Lower reach: most downstream site |
| 04 Middle | Middle | 4254966.47, 713101.21 | Consistently contains water and only reach sampled within this stream |
| 05 Middle | | | Remove from monitoring due to lack of water |
| 10 Middle<br>10 Upper | Middle | 4254565.19, 715113.34 | Middle reach: consistently contains water |
| 12 Middle | Middle | 4255010.98, 718023.53 | Consistently contains water and only reach sampled within this stream |
| 17 Lower<br>17 Upper | Upper | 4263400.48, 710480.77 | Upper reach: consistently contains water |
| 18 Middle | | | Remove from monitoring due to lack of water |
| 22 Lower<br>22 Left Upper<br>22 Right Upper | Lower | 4259710.35, 713002.62 | Lower reach: most downstream site |

Table 2 (continued). List of stream reaches retained for sampling in this protocol along with UTM coordinates (NAD83 (Conus), Zone 14 N) and justification for including each reach. Those reaches shaded in gray will no longer be monitored because they are often dry during the sampling period.

| Stream Reaches Previously Sampled | Reaches to be Retained | UTM (Northing, Easting) | Justification |
|---|---|---|---|
| 23 Middle | Middle | 4257614.80, 709898.14 | Contains Topeka shiners and only reach sampled within this stream |
| 24 Lower<br>24 Middle | Lower | 4253659.26, 710868.26 | Lower reach: most downstream site |
| 34 Lower | Lower | 4263286.45, 709866.69 | Consistently contains water and only reach sampled within stream |
| 36 Middle<br>36 Upper | Middle | 4263176.10, 710907.56 | Middle reach: downstream most site |
| 35 Lower (Fox Creek) | Lower | 4256985.51, 713944.53 | Added due to lack of information on fish communities in Fox Creek |
| **HOME**<br><br>Cub Creek Lower<br>Cub Creek Upper | Lower 4462 | 337.67, 684059.84 | Lower reach: downstream most site |

Table 3. Streams sampled at GWCA, EFMO, HEHO, HOSP, PERI, and WICR.

| Park | Streams Sampled |
|---|---|
| EFMO | Dousman Creek |
| GWCA | Carver Creek<br>Harkins Branch<br>Williams Branch |
| HEHO | Hoover Creek |
| HOSP | Bull Bayou<br>Gulpha Creek |
| PERI | Pratt Creek |
| WICR | Skegg's Branch<br>Terrell Creek<br>Wilson's Creek |

## Temporal design

Streams in PIPE and TAPR will be sampled annually because of continued interest in monitoring Topeka shiner populations in those parks (Table 4). Sampling will be done between late August and October to avoid the breeding season of the Topeka shiner. This approach is consistent with Peitz and Rowell (2004) and will allow comparisons with the historic data.

Streams in parks where Topeka Shiner populations have not been documented—EFMO, GWCA, HEHO, HOME, HOSP, PERI, and WICR—will be sampled once every three years (Table 4). The index period of sampling is based on the period of low flow conditions and co-visitation for invertebrate sampling.

Table 4. Revisit design and index period for fish monitoring in small streams of HTLN.

| Study Park | Revisit Notation | % of Annual Effort | Index Period | 2007 | 2008 | 2009 | 2010 | 2011 | 2012 | 2013 | 2014 | 2015 | 2016 | 2017 | 2018 |
|---|---|---|---|---|---|---|---|---|---|---|---|---|---|---|---|
| PIPE – TAPR- | [1-0] | 50% | August-October | X | X | X | X | X | X | X | X | X | X | X | X |
| GWCA-WICR- | [1-2] | 50% | May - June | X | | | X | | | X | | | X | | |
| EFMO-HEHO-HOME | [1-2] | 50% | July - Aug | | X | | | X | | | X | | | X | |
| PERI-HOSP | [1-2] | 50% | May - June | | | X | | | X | | | X | | | X |

## Response Design

### *Fish*

Fish community data will be used to assess overall stream quality and biotic integrity of these small streams. At PIPE, TAPR, and HOME fish collection methods generally follow Peitz and Rowell (2004) to allow for comparisons with historical data. Collection of fish data at EFMO, GWCA, HEHO, HOSP, PERI, and WICR follows Petersen *et al.* (2008). Within each reach, data on the entire fish community will be collected including: community composition (species richness and percent composition of each species), abundance (catch per effort) size structure (lengths and weights), and overall health (occurrence of diseases and anomalies). Fish collection and processing techniques are described in SOP #4 (Fish Community Sampling) and details on parameters used to assess biotic integrity are discussed in SOP #9 (Data Analysis).

## Habitat and Water Quality

Habitat incorporates all aspects of physical and chemical constituents and their interactions. Habitat composition within a stream is an important component in shaping aquatic communities. The type and abundance of specific habitats (*i.e.*, riffles, pools, woody debris, etc.) will influence species presence and relative abundance, as well as size structure, of the populations. Because of its importance, physical habitat data will be collected as part of this protocol to examine relationships between environmental conditions and fish communities. Variables such as current velocity; substrate size; embeddedness; water chemistry; and presence of periphyton, filamentous algae and aquatic plants play key roles in the microhabitat structure and distribution of fish. Other habitat variables such as woody debris, boulders, canopy cover, and bank condition (*e.g.*, height, angle, dominant substrate, degree of undercut, and vegetative cover) also are important for assessing stream condition. We propose to monitor all of the aforementioned habitat variables at our sampling reaches. For details on sampling physical habitat and water quality, see SOP #5 (Physical Habitat) and SOP #3 (Documenting CORE 5 Water Quality Variables).

## Rationale for the Sampling Design

Biomonitoring methodologies are constantly being developed and refined in an effort to achieve the most efficient and effective assessments of water quality, physical habitat, and fish communities. Several different sampling approaches or protocols have been used by state and federal agencies to quantify status and trends of fish communities in streams. Rapid Bioassessment Protocols (RBPs) developed by the US Environmental Protection Agency (USEPA) have been used by many agencies to evaluate fish communities in streams (Barbour *et al.*, 1999). These protocols are designed to give a quick, broad picture of stream quality and fish assemblages throughout a region with minimal field and laboratory efforts. Additional and commonly used monitoring protocols include the EPA Environmental Monitoring and Assessment Program (EMAP) protocols for wadeable streams (Lazorchak *et al.*, 1998; McCormick and Hughes, 1998), and the USGS NAWQA protocols (Moulton *et al.*, 2002). In comparison to the RPBs, these latter two protocols involve more rigorous data collection (*i.e.*, collection of fish lengths and weights) and quantitative methods (*i.e.*, designated reach length), giving a more complete picture of fish assemblage composition and structure.

The many streams monitored in this protocol are located in different physiographic regions (Central Lowlands, Ozark Plateaus, and Ouachita Province) with varying stream geomorphology, sediment composition, and riparian vegetation. Therefore, this protocol is a combination of the original fish protocol (Peitz and Rowell, 2004) established for softer sediment prairie streams and the HTLN river fish protocol (Petersen *et al.*, 2008) established for Ozark rivers and tributaries with larger sediment. To maintain comparability with historic monitoring data at PIPE, TAPR, and HOME, a modified version of the original prairie fish protocol will be used. These modifications bring this original fish protocol in line with other national-level protocols (NAWQA and EMAP) by focusing on the entire community and sampling all available habitats throughout the reach. The sampling approach described in this protocol for EFMO, GWCA, HEHO, PERI, HOSP, and WICR is based on methods in the HTLN river fish protocol, a modified NAWQA protocol. It was necessary to modify the NAWQA fish protocol for both this protocol and the HTLN river fish protocol to meet specific objectives of the HTLN long-term monitoring program. Reach selection in this protocol is similar to that of tributaries sampled under the HTLN river fish protocol in that one reach per stream is sampled at the downstream end of the watershed due to the relatively short length (≤3 km) of all the streams included in this protocol. The one difference in reach selection between this protocol and the HTLN river fish protocol is that the downstream boundary of the reach is based on professional judgment and co-location with other monitoring programs (similar to NAWQA reach selection methods); whereas, the HTLN river fish protocol uses location of the second riffle upstream of the floodplain for establishing the downstream reach boundary. Because some of the streams under this protocol have primarily run/pool morphology, we can not use location of riffles to establish the downstream reach boundary for all streams in all parks.

# III. Field and Laboratory Methods

## Field Season Preparations, Field Schedule, and Equipment Setup

Procedures for field season preparations, including preparation of a field sampling schedule and equipment setup, are described in SOP #1 (Preparation for Field Sampling). The project leader (fisheries biologist) will ensure that team members have read and understand the protocol and supporting SOPs prior to sampling and that all required equipment and supplies have been ordered and are in proper working condition. Fieldwork must be scheduled in advance so that crews can be assigned. Training team members on use of fish sampling and water quality meters will be completed prior to field work (see SOP #2). Time spent at a sampling reach will vary, but anywhere from 2 – 4 hours per reach is typical. Sampling period will vary depending on the park to be sampled (see index period in Table 4). The project leader will prepare and maintain a field notebook detailing all sampling-related activities and staff participation during monitoring trips to ensure that trip reports are complete and accurate. Finally, the project leader will ensure that all required scientific collection permits have been obtained.

## Collecting Fish Samples

At PIPE, TAPR, and HOME, fish community data will be collected at three to five sites (channel units) within each sample reach using a minnow seine (Figure 1). Single pass electrofishing methods will be employed throughout each sampling reach at EFMO, GWCA, HEHO, HOSP, PERI, and WICR (Figure 2).The size of the stream (width and depth) will determine the size of seine used or the type of electrofishing gear used (tow barge versus backpack electrofisher). Associated habitat and water quality will be measured in conjunction with fish sampling at all parks.

## Historically Sampled Parks
### (seining methods)

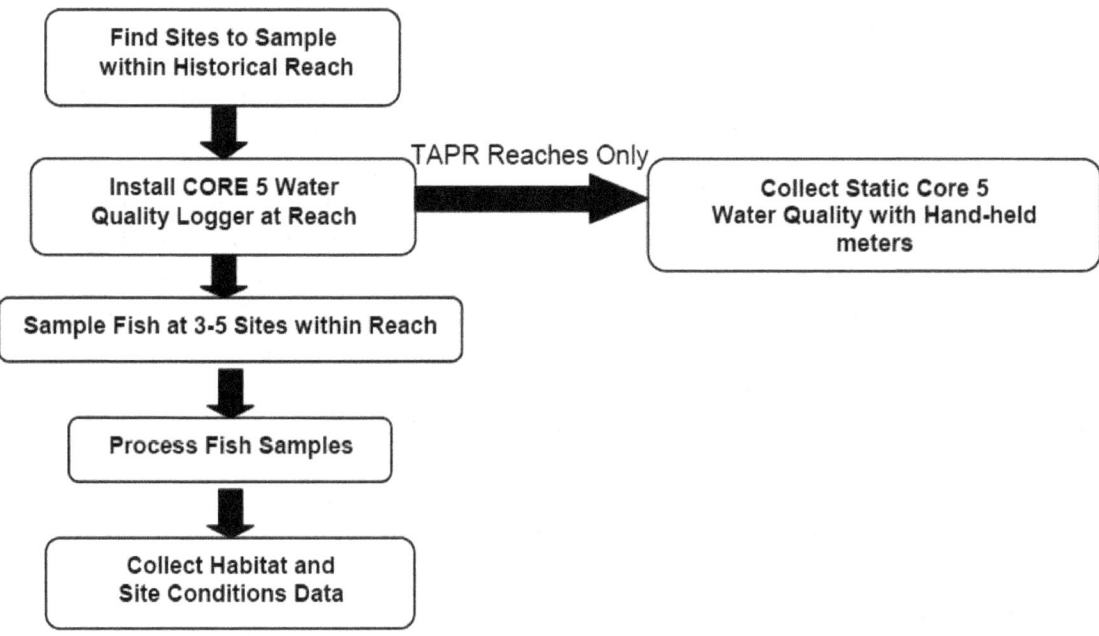

Figure 1. Flow of work diagram for parks sampled by seining under the original prairie fish protocol.

## Additional Parks
### (electrofishing methods)

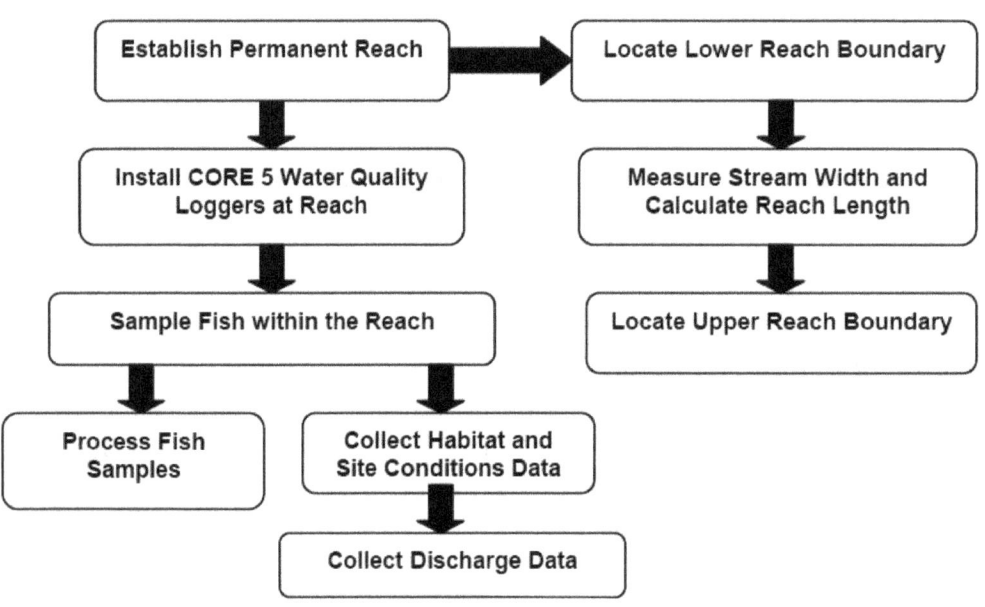

Figure 2. Flow of work diagram for added parks using electrofishing methods.

When monitoring, it is important to note that gear type and efficiency have been shown to affect data quality obtained from fish community sampling. In a study of fish data from 55 NAWQA sites, Meador and McIntyre (2003) found that among electrofishing methods (backpack, towed barge, and boat), Jaccard's (similarity) index and percent similarity index values between years and between multiple reaches were significantly greater for backpack electrofishing. These results suggest that data collected using different gear types (or different combinations of multiple types of gear) may be subject to considerable variability. Because this protocol is concerned with monitoring temporal changes within each stream reach rather than comparing across streams that may have been sampled using different gears, it is imperative to maintain consistency among gear type and sampling effort in the reaches across years (see Table 5).

During sample processing, the gear used, time spent sampling, length of the reach or site sampled, and species data will be recorded. To the extent practical, individual specimens will be identified to species in the field using appropriate fish identification keys and other relevant information. Specimens that cannot be reliably identified in the field will be preserved for later identification in the laboratory (see SOP #4). Individual lengths and weights will be collected on a subsample of each species at a reach to estimate the size structure and community composition. Anomalies will also be recorded to determine the occurrence of diseases and deformities in the fish populations.

Table 5. List of stream reaches sampled for fish communities and list of gear used and percent effort by gear for each reach.

| Park | Streams Sampled | Gear Type Used | % Effort by Gear |
|---|---|---|---|
| EFMO | Dousman Creek | Backpack Electrofisher | 100 |
| GWCA | Carver Creek<br>Harkins Branch<br>Williams Branch | Backpack Electrofisher<br>Backpack Electrofisher<br>Backpack Electrofisher | 100<br>100<br>100 |
| HEHO | Hoover Creek | Backpack Electrofisher | 100 |
| HOME | Cub Creek | Seine | 100 |
| HOSP | Bull Bayou<br>Gulpha Creek | Backpack Electrofisher<br>Backpack Electrofisher | 100<br>100 |
| PERI | Pratt Creek | Backpack Electrofisher | 100 |
| PIPE | Pipestone Creek | Seine | 100 |
| TAPR | 12 streams | Seine | 100 |
| WICR | Skegg's Branch<br>Terrell Creek<br>Wilson's Creek | Backpack Electrofisher Backpack<br>Electrofisher<br>Towed Barge Electrofisher | 100<br>100<br>100 |

**Measuring CORE 5 Water Quality and Physical Habitat**

CORE 5 water quality parameters (temperature, dissolved oxygen, specific conductance, pH, and turbidity) will be recorded using a data logger or sonde at each reach. The data logger will be deployed in or near the sampling reach and allowed to operate for a minimum of 48 hours. Instructions for using the datalogger are located in SOP #3 (Documenting CORE 5 Water Quality Variables). Due to the large number of reaches at TAPR, deployment of data loggers at each reach is not practical, and static CORE 5 will be taken at most sampling sites using hand-held meters. However, data loggers will be deployed at selected reaches at TAPR to collect continuous data. Discharge will be measured only at reaches sampled by electrofishing gear. Instructions for measuring stream discharge are in SOP #6 (Measuring Stream Discharge).

Habitat composition will be measured in conjunction with fish sampling. For PIPE, TAPR, and HOME, methods are modified from Peitz and Rowell (2004). For the remaining parks, habitat methods follow Petersen *et al.* (2008). For all nine parks, physical habitat is assessed at transects perpendicular to flow. At each transect, several physical attributes will be measured including width, depth, velocity, in-stream substrate, bank erosion/stability, and riparian cover. See SOP #5 for details on habitat collection methods.

**Sample Storage and Reference Collection**

A reference collection of identified fish species is kept at the NPS HTLN office located at Missouri State University, Springfield, Missouri. All other fish collected during monitoring will be returned to the streams from which they were collected or disposed of properly.

**Post Season Procedures**

Procedures for the end of the sample season are found in SOP #7 (Procedures and Equipment Storage after the Field Season).

# IV. Data Management

## Overview of Database Design

Effective data management allows the project leader to store and retrieve large quantities of data securely and efficiently. Data management especially becomes an issue when observational sample sizes are in the range of $10^4$ to $10^5$ or greater. Database design is critical to understanding how to use a database effectively. All data management activities related to this protocol are described in more detail in SOP #8 (Data Management).

The Inventory and Monitoring (I&M) Program designed the Natural Resource Database Template (NRDT) as a proof-of-concept database model for managing long-term ecological monitoring data. Two widely-distributed versions have been implemented in Access (NPS, 2006). The database template has a core structure that standardizes the relationship between location and temporal data. The template promotes integration of I&M datasets and reduces database development time.

The NPS Water Resource Division designed the NPStoret database to facilitate archiving NPS water quality data in the EPA Storet database. The database includes a sophisticated user interface, data-entry templates, and an import module for loading NRDT-style data sources. These features are specifically designed to share water quality data across natural resource agencies.

Microsoft Access 2003 is the primary software environment for managing the small streams fish community and habitat data. ArcGIS 9.2 (Environmental Systems Research Institute, Inc.) is used for managing spatial data associated with field sampling locations. Data and metadata products will be posted at the NPS I&M website, http://science.nature.nps.gov/nrgis/, and EPA Storet National Data Warehouse. QA/QC guidelines in this document are based on recommendations of Rowell *et al.* (2005) and S. Fancy at http://science.nature.nps.gov/im/monitor/index.cfm and citations therein.

The database for small stream fish monitoring has a hierarchical design based on NRDT. Locations (reaches) and sampling periods are maintained at the top level of the database. This database is the product of two other databases linked together by location and sampling season. The databases represent two field sampling methods, seining and electrofishing. Currently, sampling at PIPE, TAPR, and HOME is limited to seining, while electrofishing is used at EFMO, GWCA, HEHO, HOSP, PERI, and WICR.

These differences, from the point-of-view of data management, include:

(1) Seining tables include multiple sampling sites (up to five) within a reach. Tables and their relationships for seining data management originate from the legacy database "Shiner" that addressed prairie streams and the federally listed Topeka shiner (Peitz and Rowell, 2004). Modified fish sampling and habitat procedures included in this protocol are represented in the new seining database. Among the new features are the inclusion of individually measured fish attributes (total length, weight, anomalies, etc.) and the addition of physical attributes taken at the site level (site dimensions and streambank erosion percent). Each of the original tables from "Shiner" has been included and it is possible to integrate each table into data exports for analysis.

(2) Electrofishing locations represent the reach level. Tables and their relationships for electro-fish data management are drawn from the design used in the HTLN river fish protocol (Petersen *et al.*, 2008).

The general data model for fish community monitoring consists of two core sets of tables. One set manages species attribute data (species names, lengths, weights, counts, *etc.*) and the other associated habitat data. Species attribute and habitat data are linked in time and space by way of standardized location and date tables. The primary table for storing species attribute data contains information about the species. Supporting tables include taxonomic information, observers, and equipment information. A locations table provides detailed location information associated with each sampling reach. Look-up tables are linked to relevant tables to provide the values for pick-lists on data-entry forms, thereby reducing possible error during data entry (see Data Verification and Editing below).

## Data Entry

A number of features have been designed into the database to minimize errors that occur when field data are transcribed to the database for storage and analysis. Forms are used as portals for data entry into the database. Standardized identifiers (*e.g.*, sample location and periods) are selected from a list of easily interpreted codes. Species and habitat data are entered into fields linked to appropriate tables. Look-up tables contain project-specific data and prohibit entry of data into a field if a corresponding value is not included in the look-up table. Consequently, only valid names or measures may be entered and spelling mistakes are eliminated. Species or habitat measures are selected using a pick list or by typing the beginning of the name.

## Data Verification and Editing

Data verification immediately follows data entry and involves checking the accuracy of computerized records against the original source, usually paper field records. While the goal of data entry is to achieve 100% correct entries, this is rarely accomplished. To minimize transcription errors, our policy is to verify 100% of records to their original source by staff familiar with project design and field implementation. Further, 10% of records are reviewed a second time by the project leader and the results of that comparison reported with the data. If errors are found in the project leader's review, then the entire data set is verified again. Once the computerized data are verified as accurately reflecting the original field data, the paper forms are archived and the electronic version is used for all subsequent data activities.

Although data may be correctly transcribed from the original field forms, they may not be accurate or logical. For example, a fish count of 2,377 instead of 237 may be illogical and almost certainly incorrect, whether or not it was properly transcribed from field forms. The process of reviewing computerized data for range and logic errors is the validation stage. Certain components of data validation are built into data entry forms (*e.g.*, range limits). Data validation can also be extended into the design and structure of the database. As much as possible, values for data-entry forms have been limited to valid entries stored in the look-up tables.

Additional data validation can be accomplished during verification, if the operator is sufficiently knowledgeable about the data. The project leader will validate the data after verification is complete. Validation procedures seek to identify generic errors (*e.g.*, missing, mismatched, or duplicate records) as well as errors specific to particular projects.

During the entry, verification, and validation phases, the project leader is responsible for the data. The project leader must assure consistency between field forms and the database by noting how and why any changes were made to the data on the original field forms. In general, changes made to the field forms should not be made via erasure, but rather through marginal notes or attached explanations. Once validation is complete, the data set is turned over to the data manager for archiving and storage.

Spatial validation of database sample coordinates can be accomplished using ArcGIS (ESRI, Inc.). Because this is an Access-maintained database, it can be converted into a geodatabase with ArcCatalog (ArcGIS, ESRI, Inc.). Coordinate data (UTM northing and easting) of the locations table can then be used to validate the UTM coordinate values for sample locations stored in Access against the original GPS coordinates.

## Metadata Procedures

Metadata for project data are developed in XML format using NPS Metadata Tools and Editor. These software tools provide a basic stylesheet that follows current Federal Geographic Data Committee (FGDC) standards. In addition, they provide enhanced displays for biological and natural resource information metadata and upload/download network tools for managing metadata between the local workstation and WASO Natural Resource GIS server.

## Database Versions

Changes in database structure and functionality require a versioning system. This allows for the tracking of changes over time. With proper controls and communication, versioning ensures that only the most current version is used in any analysis. Versioning of archived data sets is handled by adding a two digit number separated by a period to the file name, with the first version being numbered 1.0. Minor changes such as revisions in forms and report content should be noted by an increase of the number to the right of the period. Major changes such as migration between Access versions or database normalization across multiple tables should be indicated by an increase in the number to the left of the period. Frequent users of the data are notified of the updates, and provided with a copy of the most recent archived version.

## Database Security

Secure data archiving is essential for protecting data files from corruption. No versions of the database should be deleted under any circumstance. Multiple backup copies of all program data are maintained at the HTLN offices, at the Wilson's Creek visitor center, and at the Missouri State University campus offices. Tape backups of the databases are made weekly. Each weekly full backup copy is maintained at the Wilson's Creek National Battlefield Visitor Center, Republic, MO. Once a month, one tape copy is stored offsite.

Currently, data are available for research and management applications on request, for database versions where all QA/QC has been completed and the data have been archived. Most data requests are currently met using FTP services. Portions of the monitoring data collected under this protocol will be made available for download directly from the NPS I&M Monitoring webpage. Information related to location and persistence of species determined to be threatened or endangered will not be made available for download by the general public. Data requests should be directed to:

Data Manager
Heartland I&M Network
National Park Service
Wilson's Creek National Battlefield
6424 W. Farm Road 182
Republic, MO 65738-9514
(417) 732-6438

# V. Analysis and Reporting

## Metric Calculations for Fish Communities

Several parameters and analysis techniques have been used to detect trends in fish communities and investigate the relationships between fish communities and environmental conditions. Biological metrics are commonly used by scientists to compare the condition of the biological community at multiple sites (Simon, 1999) or across time. A metric is a characteristic of the biota that changes in a predictable way with increased human disturbance (Barbour *et al.*, 1999). Attributes of the fish community such as habitat and substrate preferences, trophic guilds, spawning preferences, and degree of tolerance to disturbance are measures frequently reflected in metrics making it possible to determine relationships between biological communities and environmental conditions. Metrics that are commonly used by biologists to detect trends in fish communities-such as species richness, diversity, abundance, and community composition-will be calculated at all parks.

An extension of the metric approach is to combine multiple metrics into an Index of Biotic Integrity (IBI). This index is used as an indicator of overall stream quality, enabling investigators to compare conditions at multiple sites (Karr, 1981; Barbour *et al.*, 1999; Simon, 1999) or at a single site across time. Prior to using fish communities as bioindicators, aquatic invertebrate communities were (and still are) used as indicators of stream quality (Hilsenhoff, 1977). The popularity of fish with the general public and stakeholders has made them the most commonly used bioindicator for investigating ecological relationships using the IBI approach in streams (Barbour *et al.*, 1999; Simon, 1999).

One of the first fish IBIs developed by Karr (1981) has been modified for use in rivers and streams in many other regions and countries (Fausch *et al.*, 1984; Hughes and Oberdorff, 1998; Simon, 1999). Some IBIs have been specifically designed for particular states such as Illinois (Smogor, 2005), Ohio (Yoder and Smith, 1999), Wisconsin (Lyons *et al.*, 1996), and Missouri (Matt Combes, Missouri Department of Conservation, written comm., 2006). Others have been created or modified for use in larger regions such as the Midwest (Fausch *et al.*, 1984), the Ozark Highlands (Dauwalter *et al.*, 2003), and the Ouachita Mountains Ecoregion (Hlass *et al.*, 1998). Parks monitored under this protocol are located in various geologic ecoregions and states. Therefore, we will assess the applicability of state and regional IBIs for use at each park. A detailed summary of calculated metrics and data analyses are given in SOP #9 (Data Analysis).

## Data Analysis

In determining the appropriate statistical approaches for this monitoring protocol, it is important to take into account the primary audience of the various reports that will result. This audience primarily consists of park resource managers, park superintendents, and other park staff. Park resource managers and staff may not have an in-depth background in statistical methods, and park superintendents may have limited time to devote to such reports. Additionally, protocols such as this may provide much data on many different types of variables. Thus it is important, to the extent possible, that the core data analyses and presentation methods provide a standard format for evaluation of numerous variables, are relatively straightforward to interpret, can be quickly updated whenever additional data become available, and can be used for many different types of indicators, whether univariate or multivariate. Additionally, the type and magnitude of variability or uncertainty associated with the results should be easily discernible, and a threshold for potential management action ideally will be indicated.

Most formal statistical tests involve a null hypothesis of no difference or no change. The problem with such approaches is that the hypothesis under test is thus trivial (Cherry, 1998; Johnson, 1999; Anderson *et al.*, 2000, 2001). No populations or communities will be exactly the same at different times. Thus, the magnitude of change and its biological importance is of primary interest rather than change per se. Null hypothesis significance testing relies heavily on *P*-values, and results primarily in yes – no decisions (reject or fail to reject the null hypothesis). *P*-values are strongly influenced by sample size, however, and one may, with a large enough sample size, obtain a statistically 'significant' result that is not biologically important. Alternatively, with a small sample size, one may determine that a biologically important result is not statistically significant (Yoccoz, 1991). Thus, traditional null hypothesis testing places the emphasis on the *P*-value (which is dependent on sample size) and rejection of the null hypothesis, whereas we should be more concerned whether the data reflect biologically important changes (Kirk, 1996; Hoenig and Heisey, 2001). Finally, because data are collected and summarized at the level of the reach and reaches are not replicated, many types of statistical tests will not be possible.

Parameter estimation provides more information than hypothesis testing, is more straightforward to interpret, and easier to compute (*e.g.*, Steidl *et al.*, 1997; Gerard *et al.*, 1998; Johnson, 1999; Anderson *et al.*, 2000, 2001; Colegrave and Ruxton, 2003; Nakagawa and Foster, 2004). Parameter estimation emphasizes the magnitude of effects and the biological significance of the results, rather than making binary decisions (Shaver, 1993; Stoehr, 1999). There is no formal classification of error associated with parameter estimation. Moreover, trend studies should focus on description of trends and their uncertainty, rather than hypothesis testing (Olsen *et al.*, 1997). Thus, most of the data analyses conducted under this protocol will take the form of parameter estimation, in the form of metric calculation, rather than null hypothesis significance testing.

Control charts will also be used in data organization and analysis (see SOP 9 for details). Control charts, developed for industrial applications, indicate when a system is going 'out of control', by plotting through time some measure of a stochastic process with reference to its expected value (*e.g.*, Beauregard *et al.*, 1992; Gyrna, 2001; Montgomery, 2001). Control charts may be univariate or multivariate, and can represent many different types of variables. Control charts have been applied to ecological data (McBean and Rovers, 1998; Manly, 2001), including fish communities (Pettersson, 1998; Anderson and Thompson, 2004) and natural resources within the I&M program (Atkinson *et al.*, 2003). Control charts contain upper and lower control limits specifying thresholds beyond which variability in the indicator reveals a biologically important change is occurring, and warns that management may need to act. Control limits can be set to any desired level.

Multivariate control charts may also be constructed, and although some of the above-mentioned texts describe multivariate control charts (using the Hotelling $T^2$ statistic), this approach is only practical for a small number of variables, and assumes a multivariate normal distribution. In general, species abundances are not distributed as multivariate normal (Taylor, 1961), and traditional multivariate procedures are frequently not robust to violations of this assumption (Mardia, 1971; Olson, 1974). A new type of multivariate control chart has recently been described for use with complex ecological communities and a software application entitled *ControlChart.exe* is available for constructing these types of multivariate control charts (see Anderson and Thompson, 2004). Multivariate temporal autocorrelation will violate the assumption of stochasticity upon which this method is based, however, it is important to test for temporal autocorrelation using Mantel correlograms prior to using this method. This new multivariate control chart appears to have promise but has not been widely applied nor thoroughly evaluated. Further evaluation of this method is warranted before being applied to the data of this protocol.

Although the primary approach to organizing and analyzing data will consist of metric estimation combined with the use of control charts, other statistical methods are not entirely ruled out at this time. The potential analyses techniques that could be applied are limited, however, because no true replicates are obtained for most streams. Additionally, data from fish studies are often not normally distributed. A Friedman two-way analysis of variance by ranks is a non parametric analogue of a repeated measures ANOVA that does not require replication, and thus would be well suited to this data set. If a degree of normality could be obtained (or the appropriate transformations successfully applied), a simple regression could be applied, with time as the predictor variable. Because data for most parks will only be collected at 3-year intervals, however, several decades may elapse before statistical power is adequate.

Multivariate analyses that attribute variability in community data to specific environmental variables or gradients may also be employed (Gauch, 1982; Jongman *et al.*, 1995; Everitt and Dunn, 2001; Timm, 2002). Multivariate techniques differ from univariate or bivariate analyses in that the former techniques generate a hypothesis from the biological data rather than disproving a null hypothesis, and the effectiveness improves as the number of variables increase (Williams and Gillard, 1971). Two techniques used to analyze community data include ordination and classification (Gauch, 1982; Jongman *et al.*, 1995; Everitt and Dunn, 2001; Timm, 2002).

A formal power analysis for this protocol was not conducted for three reasons: (1) The primary purpose of conducting a prospective power analysis is to determine whether the proposed sample size is adequate. Because data are collected or summarized at the level of the reach, and it is not possible or feasible to establish multiple reaches per stream at most parks, sample size could not be increased regardless of the result of any power analysis. Furthermore, in many analyses, sample size will equate with number of years; in this case, analyses will simply become more powerful over time. (2) Statistical power is dependent upon the hypothesis under test and the statistical test used. Over the course of this long-term monitoring program, there may be interest in many different questions and hypotheses that could potentially be evaluated. Thus, there is no single 'power' relevant to the overall protocol. Estimating power at this point in the context of such a long-term, multifaceted monitoring program could be potentially misleading, as the test this power is based upon may rarely (or never) actually be employed. (3) Most of data analyses under this protocol will take the form of parameter/metric calculation (for habitat parameters, associated confidence intervals or standard errors will be calculated), rather than null hypothesis significance testing. When estimating such parameters, there is no associated statistical power. In general, statistical power analyses are frequently mis-used and misinterpreted in ecological contexts (Morrison, 2007), and alternative approaches to evaluating the degree of uncertainty associated with our data will be evaluated and used when applicable.

## Reporting

For those parks sampled annually (PIPE and TAPR), reports summarizing monitoring data will be prepared each year. For those parks sampled on a rotational basis (EFMO, GWCA, HEHO, HOME, HOSP, PERI, and WICR), reports will be prepared every third year. These reports will include an update on the status of the resources in addition to documenting related data management activities and data summaries. In an effort to disseminate findings in a timely manner, annual summary reports should be completed by

May of the year following data collection. Depending on observed impacts in the watershed and how critical summary information is for setting management goals, comprehensive trends analysis and synthesis reports should be completed every five to ten years for those parks sampled annually and every nine to twelve years for those parks on rotation. Executive summaries should be prepared for all types of reports. Refer to SOP #10 (Data Reporting) for details on types of reports and their primary audiences, report structure and style, and review procedures.

# VI. Personnel Requirements and Training

## Roles and Responsibilities

The project manager/project leader is the fisheries biologist for the HTLN and this person bears responsibility for implementing this monitoring protocol. Because consistency is essential to implementation of the protocol, the project manager will usually lead field data collection efforts unless technicians have several years of experience collecting the data related to this protocol as determined by the project manager. The project manager will oversee all laboratory work including all QA/QC requirements. The data management aspect of the monitoring effort is the shared responsibility of the project manager and the data manager. Typically, the project manager is responsible for data collection, data entry, data verification and validation, data summary, analysis, and reporting. The data manager is responsible for data archiving, data security, dissemination, and database design. The data manager, in collaboration with the project manager, also develops data entry forms and other database features as part of quality assurance and automates report generation. The data manager is ultimately responsible to ensure that adequate QA/QC procedures are built into the database management system and appropriate data handling procedures followed. The program aquatic ecologists will assist the project manager with field collection and laboratory processing, equipment maintenance, purchasing of supplies, and sample storage. The fisheries biologist (or one of the aquatic ecologists with skills in taxonomic identification) will be responsible for identifying fish to the species level in the field and the laboratory.

## Qualifications and Training

Training is an essential component for collecting credible data. Training for consistency and accuracy should be emphasized for both the field and laboratory aspects of the protocol. SOP #2 (Training) describes the training requirements for new technicians. The project manager should oversee this training and ensure that each technician is adequately prepared to collect data. Taxonomic identifications for fish may be performed by a technician with several years of experience, but initial identifications should be checked by expert taxonomists.

# VII. Operational Requirements

## Annual Workload and Field Schedule

Samples will be taken once a year at PIPE and TAPR and once every three years for EFMO, GWCA, HEHO, HOME, HOSP, PERI, and WICR (see Table 4 for index period). Sampling at each park should begin approximately at the same time each year, and samples should be collected within the shortest time frame possible to minimize the effects of seasonal change. For fish monitoring a minimum crew of 3-5 will be needed depending on the gear used. For habitat sampling, a minimum of two people will be required, but three people make the process much more efficient. Typically, two to three reaches can be sampled in one day depending on ease of access and number of personnel.

## Facility and Equipment Requirements

Field and lab equipment listed in SOP #1 (Preparation for Field Sampling and Laboratory Processing) are only for one sampling crew. Beyond normal office and equipment storage space, facility needs include access to a wet laboratory.

## Startup Costs and Budget Considerations

Estimated costs for conducting fish monitoring are shown in Table 6. Personnel expenses for fieldwork are based on a crew of three to five (fisheries biologist to oversee the fieldwork, one to two aquatic ecologists and two to three seasonal biological science technicians to assist in field data collection). Assistance with field work from other agencies and park personnel is always welcome to the extent it is available. Field costs may vary somewhat from year to year depending on the skill level and size of crew and based on travel distance to those parks sampled on a rotation. Data management personnel expenses include staff time of the fisheries biologist and data manager.

Table 6. Estimated annual costs for conducting fish monitoring in small streams.

| Project Area | Estimated Costs |
|---|---|
| Personnel costs | $79,644 |
| Admin support to WICR | $1,176 |
| Overhead to MSU | $500 |
| Field work travel | $2,888 |
| Computer hardware and software | $760 |
| Vehicle lease | $1,824 |
| Field / office equipment | $1,368 |
| Supplies | $912 |
| Lab fees | $2,000 |
| **TOTAL $91,072** | |

# VIII. Procedures for Protocol Revision

Revisions to both the Protocol Narrative and to specific Standard Operating Procedures (SOPs) are to be expected. Careful documentation of changes to the protocol and a library of previous protocol versions are essential for maintaining consistency in data collection and for appropriate treatment of the data during data summary and analysis. The Microsoft Access® database for each monitoring component contains a field that identifies the protocol version used when the data were collected.

The rationale for dividing a sampling protocol into a Protocol Narrative with supporting SOPs is based on the following:

- The Protocol Narrative is a general overview of the protocol that gives the history and justification for doing the work and an overview of the sampling methods, but that does not provide all of the methodological details. The Protocol Narrative will only be revised if major changes are made to the protocol.
- SOPs, in contrast, are very specific step-by-step instructions for performing a given task. They are expected to be revised more frequently than the protocol narrative.
- When an SOP is revised it usually is not necessary to revise the Protocol Narrative to reflect the specific changes made to the SOP.
- All versions of the Protocol Narrative and SOPs will be archived in a Protocol Library.

The steps for changing the protocol are outlined in SOP #11 (Revising the Protocol). Each SOP contains a Revision History Log that should be filled out each time a SOP is revised to explain why the change was made, and to assign a new Version Number to the revised SOP. The new version of the SOP or Protocol Narrative should then be archived in the HTLN Protocol Library under the appropriate folder.

# IX. References

Anderson, D. R., K. P. Burnham, and W. L. Thompson. 2000. Null hypothesis testing: problems, prevalence, and an alternative. Journal of Wildlife Management **64**:912-923.

Anderson, D. R., W. A. Link, D. H. Johnson, and K. P. Burnham. 2001. Suggestions for presenting the results of data analyses. Journal of Wildlife Management **65**:373-378.

Anderson, M. J., and A. A. Thompson. 2004. Multivariate control charts for ecological and environmental monitoring. Ecological Applications **14**:1921-1935.

Angermeier, P.L., and J.R. Karr. 1994. Biological integrity versus biological diversity as policy directives. BioScience **44**:690-697.

Atkinson, A. J., R. N. Fisher, C. J. Rochester, and C. W. Brown. 2003. Sampling design optimization and establishment of baselines for herptofauna arrays at the Point Loma Ecological Reserve. United States Geological Survey, Western Ecological Research Center, Sacramento, CA.

Barbour, M. T., J. Gerritsen, B. D. Snyder, and J. B. Stribling. 1999. Rapid bioassessment protocols for use in streams and wadeable rivers: periphyton, benthic macroinvertebrate, and fish, 2nd edition. EPA 841-B-99-002, U.S. Environmental Protection Agency, Washington, DC.

Beauregard, M. R., R. J. Mikulak, and B. A. Olson. 1992. A practical guide to statistical quality improvement: opening up the statistical toolbox. Van Nostrand Reinhold, New York, NY.

Bosanko, D. 2007. Fish of Minnesota Field Guide. Adventure Publications, Inc., Cambridge, MN.

Carter, R.W., and J. Davidian. 1969. General procedure for gaging streams. Book 3, Chapter A6 of Techniques of water-resources investigations of the United States Geological Survey. United States Government Printing Office, Washington, DC.

CBE Style Manual Committee. 1994. Scientific style and format: the CBE manual for authors, editors, and publishers, 6th edition. Council of Biology Editors, Cambridge University Press, New York, NY.

Cherry, S. 1998. Statistical tests in publications of The Wildlife Society. Wildlife Society Bulletin **26**:947-953.

Colegrave, N., and G. D. Ruxton. 2003. Confidence intervals are a more useful complement to nonsignificant tests than are power calculations. Behavioral Ecology **14**:446-450.

Conover, W. J. 1999. Practical nonparametric statistics. John Wiley & Sons, Inc., New York, NY.

Cross, F.B., and J.T. Collins. 1995. Fishes in Kansas. Public Education Series No. 14, University of Kansas Natural History Museum, University Press of Kansas, Lawrence, KS.

Daubenmire, R.F. 1959. Canopy coverage method of vegetation analysis. Northwest Science **33**: 43-64.

Dauwalter, D.C., E. J. Pert, and W. E. Keith. 2003. An index of biotic integrity for fish assemblages in Ozark Highland Streams of Arkansas. Southeastern Naturalist **2**:447-468.

Day, R. A. and B. Gastel. 2006. How to write and publish a scientific paper, 6th edition. ISI Press, Philadelphia, PA.

DeBacker, M. D., C. C. Young (editor), P. Adams, L. Morrison, D. Peitz, G. A. Rowell, M.H. Williams, and D. Bowles. 2005. Heartland Inventory and Monitoring Network and Prairie Cluster Prototype Monitoring Program Vital Signs Monitoring Plan. National Park Service, Heartland I&M Network and Prairie Cluster Prototype Monitoring Program, Wilson's Creek National Battlefield, Republic, MO.

Dolan, C. R., and L. E. Miranda. 2004. Injury and mortality of warmwater fishes immobilized by electrofishing. North American Journal of Fisheries Management **24**:118-127.

Donegon, D.S. 1984. Wilson's Creek fish species diversity. Unpublished report.

Doppelt, B. M, C. Scurlock, and J. Karr. 1993. Entering the watershed: a new approach to save America's river ecosystems. Island Press, Washington, DC.

Everitt, B. S., and G. Dunn. 2001. Applied Multivariate Data Analysis, 2nd edition. Hodder Arnold Publishers, London, England.

Fausch, K.D., J.R. Karr, and P.R. Yant. 1984. Regional application of an index of biotic integrity based on stream fish communities. Transactions of the American Fisheries Society **113**:39-55.

Federal Register. 2002. Endangered and threatened wildlife and plants; designation of critical habitat for the Topeka shiner; proposed rule. 50 CFR Part 17, RIN 1018-AI20, Federal Register 67:54261-54262.

Fitzpatrick, F. A., I. R. Waite, P. J. D'Arconte, M. R. Meador, M. A. Maupin, and M. E. Gurtz. 1998. Revised methods for characterizing stream habitat in the National Water-Quality Assessment Program. U.S. Geological Survey Water-Resources Investigations Report 98-4052. U.S. Geological Survey, Raleigh, NC.

Foster, D. 1988. Fish survey of Wilson's Creek. National Park Service, Ozark National Scenic Riverways, Van Buren, MO.

Gauch, H. G., Jr. 1982. Multivariate analysis in community ecology. Cambridge University Press, London, England.

Gerard, P. D., D. R. Smith, and G. Weerakkody. 1998. Limits of retrospective power analysis. Journal of Wildlife Management **62**:801-807.

Goldwasser, L. 1999. A collection of grammatical points. Bulletin of the Ecological Society of America **79**:148-150.

Gyrna, F. M. 2001. Quality planning and analysis: from product development through use. McGraw-Hill Irwin, New York, NY.

Hendricks, M. L., C. H. Hocutt, and J. R. Stauffer, Jr. 1980. Monitoring of fish in lotic habitats. Pages 205-231 *in* C. H. Hocutt and J. R. Stauffer, Jr., editors. Biological monitoring of fish. Lexington Books, Lexington, MA.

Hilsenhoff, W. L. 1977. Use of arthropods to evaluate water quality of streams. Wisconsin Department of Natural Resources Technical Bulletin No.100.

Hlass, L.J., W.L.Fisher, and D.J. Turton. 1998. Use of the index of biotic integrity to assess water quality in forested stream of the Ouachita Mountains Ecoregion, Arkansas. Journal of Freshwater Biology **13**:181-192.

Hoefs, N.J. and T.P. Boyle 1990. Fish community survey, Wilson's Creek, MO. Water Resource Division, Applied Research Branch, National Park Service, Colorado State University, Fort Collins, CO.

Hoenig, J. M., and D. M. Heisey. 2001. The abuse of power: the pervasive fallacy of power calculations for data analysis. The American Statistician **55**:19-24.

Hughes, R.M., and Oberdorff, T. 1998. Applications of IBI concepts and metrics to waters outside the United States and Canada. Pages 79-93 *in* T. P. Simon, editor. Assessment and approaches for estimating biological integrity using fish assemblages. CRC Press, Boca Raton, FL.

Johnson, D. H. 1999. The insignificance of statistical significance testing. Journal of Wildlife Management **63**:763-772.

Jongman, R. H. G., C. J. F. ter Braak, and O. F. R. van Tongeren. 1995. Data analysis in community and landscape ecology. Cambridge University Press, London, England.

Karr J. R. 1981. Assessment of biotic integrity using fish communities. Fisheries **6**:21–27.

Karr, J. R. and D. R. Dudley. 1981. Ecological perspective on water quality goals. Environmental Management **5**:55-68.

Kirk, R. E. 1996. Practical significance: a concept whose time has come. Educational and Psychological Measurement **56**:746-759.

Kolar, C. S., D. M. Lodge. 2002. Ecological predictions and risk assessment for alien fishes in North America. Science **298**:1233–1236.

Lazorchak, J. M., Klemm, D. J., and D. V. Peck. 1998. Environmental monitoring and assessment program-surface waters: field operations and methods for measuring the ecological condition of wadeable streams. EPA/620/R-94/004F, U.S. Environmental Protection Agency, Washington, DC.

Lyons, J., L. Wang, and T.D. Simonson. 1996. Development and validation of an index of biotic integrity for coldwater streams in Wisconsin. North American Journal of Fisheries Management **16**:241-256.

Mack, R. N. 1986.Writing with precision, clarity, and economy. Bulletin of the Ecological Society of America **67**:31-35.

Manly, B. F. J. 2001. Statistics for environmental science and management. Chapman & Hall/CRC, Boca Raton, FL.

Mardia, K. V. 1971. The effect of nonnormality on some multivariate tests and robustness to nonnormality in the linear model. Biometrika **58**:105-121.

McBean, E. A., and F. A. Rovers. 1998. Statistical procedures for analysis of environmental monitoring data and risk assessment. Prentice Hall PTR, Upper Saddle River, NJ.

McCormick, F. H., and R. M. Hughes. 1998. Aquatic vertebrates. *in* J. M. Lazorchak, D. J. Klemm, and D. V. Peck, editors. Environmental Monitoring and Assessment Program—surface waters: field operations and methods for measuring the ecological condition of wadeable streams. U. S. Environmental Protection Agency Report, EPA 620–R–94–004F.

McMichael, G. A., A. L. Fritts, and T. N. Pearsons. 1998. Electrofishing injury to stream salmonids; injury assessment at the sample, reach, and stream scales. North American Journal of Fisheries Management **18**:894–904.

Meador, M. R., T. F. Cuffney, and M. E. Gurtz. 1993. Methods for sampling fish communities as part of the National Water-Quality Assessment Program. U.S. Geological Survey, Raleigh, NC. Open-File Report 93-104.

Meador, M. R, and J. P. McIntyre. 2003. Effects of electrofishing gear type on spatial and temporal variability in fish community sampling. Transactions of the American Fisheries Society **132**:709-716.

Montgomery, D. C. 2001. Introduction to statistical quality control. John Wiley & Sons, Inc., New York, NY.

Morrison, L.W. 2007. Assessing the reliability of ecological monitoring data: Power analysis and alternative approaches. Natural Areas Journal **24**:83-91.

Morrison, L.W. 2008. The use of control charts to interpret environmental monitoring data. Natural Areas Journal **28**:66-73.

Moulton, S. R. III, J. G. Kennen, R. M. Goldstein, and J. A. Hambrook. 2002. Revised protocols for sampling algal, invertebrate, and fish communities as part of the National Water-Quality Assessment Program. U.S. Geological Survey, Reston, VI. Open-file Report 02-150.

Nakagawa, S., and T. M. Foster. 2004. The case against retrospective power analyses with an introduction to power analysis. Acta Ethologica **7**:103-108.

National Park Service (NPS). 2006. Inventory and monitoring natural resource database template version 3.1 documentation. Natural Resource Program Center, Office of Inventory, Monitoring, and Evaluation, Fort Collins, CO.

National Park Service - Water Resources Division (NPS-WRD). 2003. Vital signs long term monitoring projects: part C draft guidance on WRD required and other field parameter measurements, general monitoring methods and some design considerations in preparation of a detailed study plan, accessed March, 2007 http://www.nature.nps.gov/water/VitalSigns_index/VitalSignsdocuments.cfm

National Park Service - Water Resources Division (NPS-WRD). 2007. NPStoret. http://www.nature.nps.gov/water/infoanddata/index.cfm#NPSTORET.

Ohio Environmental Protection Agency (Ohio EPA). 1987. Biological criteria for the protection of aquatic life—standardized biological field sampling and laboratory methods for assessing fish and macroinvertebrate communities. Ohio EPA, Division of Water Quality Monitoring and Assessment, Columbus, OH.

Olsen, T., B. P. Hayden, A. M. Ellison, G. W. Oehlert, and S. R. Esterby. 1997. Ecological resource monitoring: change and trend detection workshop report. Bulletin of the Ecological Society of America **78**:11-13.

Olson, C.L. 1974. Comparative robustness of six tests in multivariate analysis of variance. Journal of the American Statistical Association **69**:894-908.

Osborne, L.L., and D.A. Kovacic. 1993. Riparian vegetated buffer strips in water-quality restoration and stream management. Freshwater Biology **29**:243-258.

Peitz, D.G. 2005. Fish community monitoring in prairie park streams with emphasis on Topeka Shiner (*Notropis Topeka*): summary report 2001-2004. National Park

Service, Heartland I&M Network and Prairie Cluster Prototype Monitoring Program, Wilson's Creek National Battlefield, Republic, MO.

Peitz, D.G. and G.A. Rowell. 2004. Fish community monitoring in prairie streams with emphasis on Topeka Shiner (*Notropis Topeka*). National Park Service, Prairie Cluster Prototype Monitoring Program, Wilson's Creek National Battlefield, Republic, MO.

Peterjohn, W.T., and D.L. Correll. 1984. Nutrient dynamics in an agricultural watershed: observations on the role of a riparian forest. Ecology **65**:1466-1475.

Petersen, J.C. and B.G. Justus. 2005a. The fishes of Hot Springs National Park, Arkansas, 2003. U.S. Geological Survey, Little Rock AR. Scientific Investigations Report 2005-5126.

Petersen, J.C. and B.G. Justus. 2005b. The fishes of Wilson's Creek National Battlefield, Missouri, 2003. U.S. Geological Survey, Little Rock, AR. Scientific Investigations Report 2005-5127.


Petersen, J.C. and B.G. Justus. 2005c. The fishes of George Washington Carver National Monument, Missouri, 2003. U.S. Geological Survey, Little Rock, AR. Scientific Investigations Report 2005-5128.

Petersen, J.C. and B.G. Justus. 2005d. The fishes of Pea Ridge National Military Park, Arkansas, 2003. U.S. Geological Survey, Little Rock, AR. Scientific Investigations Report 2005-5126.

Petersen, J.C., B.G. Justus, H.R. Dodd, D.E. Bowles, L.W. Morrison, M.H. Williams, G.A. Rowell. 2008. Protocol for monitoring fish communities of Buffalo National River and Ozark National Scenic Riverways in the Ozark Plateaus of Arkansas and Missouri: Version 1.0. U.S. Geological Survey, Little Rock, AR. Open-File Report 2007-1302.

Pettersson, M. 1998. Monitoring a freshwater fish population: Statistical surveillance of biodiversity. Environmetrics **9**:139-150.

Pflieger, W. L. 1997. The fishes of Missouri. Missouri Department of Conservation. Jefferson City, MO.

Richards, C., L.B. Johnson, and G.E. Host. 1996. Landscape-scale influences on stream habitats and biota. Canadian Journal of Fisheries and Aquatic Sciences **53**:295-311.

Robins, C. R., R. M. Bailey, C. E. Bond, J. R. Brooker, E. A. Lachner, R. N. Lea, and W. B. Scott. 1991. Common and scientific names of fishes from the United States and Canada. American Fisheries Society, Special Publication 20, Bethesda, MD.

Robison, H. W., and T. M. Buchanan. 1988. Fishes of Arkansas, University of Arkansas Press, Fayetteville, AR.

Roman, S. 2002. Access Database: design and programming. O'Reilly Media. Sebastapol, CA.

Roth, N. E., J. D. Allen, and D. L. Erickson. 1996. Landscape influences on stream biotic integrity assessed at multiple spatial scales. Landscape Ecology **11**:141-156.

Rowell, G.A., and M.H. Williams. 2007. Standard Operating Procedure: WICR Heartland Network System Backups. Heartland Inventory and Monitoring Network. Wilson's Creek National Battlefield, Republic, MO.

Rowell, G. A., M. H. Williams, and M. D. DeBacker. 2005. Heartland I&M Network Data Management Plan. National Park Service. Wilson's Creek National Battlefield. Republic, MO.

Sanders, R. E., R. J. Miltner, C. O. Yoder, and E. T. Rankin. 1999. The use of external deformities, erosion, lesions, and tumors (DELT anomalies) in fish assemblages for characterizing aquatic resources—a case study of seven Ohio streams. *in*, T. P. Simon, editor. Assessing the sustainability and biological integrity of water resources using fish communities. CRC Press, New York, NY.

Shaver, J. P. 1993. What statistical significance testing is, and what it is not. Journal of Experimental Education **61**:293-316.

Simon T.P. 1999. Assessing the Sustainability and Biological Integrity of Water Resources Using Fish Communities. CRC Press, Inc., Boca Raton, FL.

Smith, P.W. 1979. The fishes of Illinois. University of Illinois Press, Urbana, IL.

Smogor, R. 2005. Draft manual for interpreting Illinois fish IBI scores. Illinois Environmental Protection Agency, Bureau of Water, Surface Water Section.

Stauffer, J.C. R.M. Goldstein, and R.M. Newman. 2000. Relationship of wooded riparian zones and runoff potential to fish community composition in agricultural streams. Canadian Journal of Fisheries and Aquatic Sciences **57**:307-316.

Steidl, R. J., J. P. Hayes, and E. Schauber. 1997. Statistical power analysis in wildlife research. Journal of Wildlife Research **61**:270-279.

Stoehr, A. M. 1999. Are significance thresholds appropriate for the study of animal behaviour? Animal Behaviour **57**:F22-F25.

Strunk, W. Jr., and E. B. White. 1999. The elements of style, 4th edition.  Macmillan, New York, NY.

Tabor, V.M.  1998.  Endangered and threatened wildlife and plants; final rule to list the Topeka shiner as endangered.  Federal Register.  **63**:69008-69021.

Taylor, L. R. 1961. Aggregation, variance, and the mean.  Nature **189**:732-735.

Timm, N. H. 2002. Applied multivariate analysis.  University of Pittsburgh Press, Pittsburg, PA.

U.S. Environmental Protections Agency (USEPA). 1990. The quality of our nation's water: a summary of the 1988 National Water Quality Inventory. EPA 440/4-90-005. U. S. Environmental Protection Agency, Washington, D. C.

U.S. Environmental Protections Agency (USEPA).  1995.  National water quality inventory: 1994 report to Congress. EPA 841-R-95-005. United States Environmental Protection Agency, Washington, D. C.

U.S. Environmental Protections Agency (USEPA). 2007. STORET Data Warehouse.  http://www.epa.gov/storet/dw_home.html

Van Sickle, J. 1997. Using mean similarity dendrograms to evaluate classifications. Journal of Agricultural, Biological, and Environmental Statistics **2**:370-388.

Wagner, R. J., R. W. Boulger, Jr., C. J. Oblinger, and B. A. Smith. 2006. Guidelines and standard procedures for continuous water-quality monitors: station operation, record computation, and data reporting.  U.S. Geological Survey Techniques and Methods 1–D3, U.S. Geological Survey, Reston, VA.

Wang, L., J. Lyons, P. Kanehl, and R. Gatti. 1997. Influence of watershed land use on habitat quality and biotic integrity in Wisconsin streams. Fisheries **22**:6-12.

Weigel, B.M., J. Lyons, L.K. Paine, S.I. Dodson, and D.J. Undersander. 2000. Using stream macroinvertebrates to compare riparian land use practices on cattle farms in southwestern Wisconsin. Journal of Freshwater Ecology. **15**:93-106.

Wentworth, C. K. 1922. A scale of grade and class terms for clastic sediments.  Journal of Geology **30**:377-392.

Williams, W.T., and P. Gillard. 1971. Pattern analysis of a grazing experiment. Australian Journal of Agricultural Research **22**:245-260.

Yoccoz, N. G. 1991. Use, overuse, and misuse of significance tests in evolutionary biology and ecology. Bulletin of the Ecological Society of America **72**:106-111.

Yoder, C.O., and M.A. Smith. 1999. Using fish assemblages in a state biological assessment and criteria program: essential concepts and considerations. Pages 17-56 *in* T.P. Simon, editor. Assessing the sustainability and biological integrity of water resources using fish communities. CRC Press, Inc., Boca Raton, FL.

# X. Standard Operating Procedures (SOPs)

## Protocol for Monitoring Fish Communities in Small Streams in the Heartland Inventory and Monitoring Network

### SOP 1: Preparation for Field Sampling

### Version 1.00 (05/01/2008)

**Revision History Log:**

| Previous Version # | Revision Date | Author | Changes Made | Reason for Change | New Version # |
|---|---|---|---|---|---|
|  |  |  |  |  |  |
|  |  |  |  |  |  |
|  |  |  |  |  |  |
|  |  |  |  |  |  |
|  |  |  |  |  |  |

This SOP provides information to prepare for the field season, including lists required of field and laboratory equipment. It also provides information on keeping records of staff time spent on sampling trips, checking water levels at the parks, and obtaining collecting permits. A list of required data sheets with a brief explanation of their purpose is provided.

## I. General Preparations

Prior to the field season all crew members should review the entire protocol, including SOPs. The following list includes key points to consider in preparing for the upcoming field season.

1. The team leader (the fisheries biologist) must prepare a field notebook for the survey year. The notebook should contain entries for observer names, field hours, and unique happenings that may influence how the data is reported. Information included in trip reports is based on what is recorded in field notebooks, so it is imperative that they are clearly organized for ease of field note entry. Notebook entries should be recorded daily to ensure accuracy. An example of a notebook log is shown in Figure 1.

| Date | Travel time (hours) | Field time (hours) | Non-project time (hours) | Lunch (hours) |
|---|---|---|---|---|
| 30 Sep 2006 | 3 | 8 | 0 | 0.5 |
| 1 Oct 2006 | 0 | 8 | 1 | 0.5 |
| 2 Oct 2006 | 3 | 8 | 0 | 0.5 |
| Notes: J. Smith and H. Simpson traveled to TAPR to conduct fish monitoring. Field assistance was provided by B. Jones and K. Adams. Returned to headquarters. Non-project time included discussing other projects with Park staff. | | | | |

Figure 1. Example of a field note book for recording scheduling, travel and field time, and personnel information.

2. Inclement weather and personnel workloads will preclude the scheduling of sampling events to specific annual dates. Sampling dates should be scheduled and logistics organized prior to the start of each field season. Monitoring efforts will require a three to five person crew depending on the gear necessary to sample fish at a park. Typically two to three reaches can be sampled in one day. Depending on the travel distance from HTLN offices to the park to be sampled, a day may be required for traveling to the park.

3. Equipment from the list below will be organized and made ready for the field season several weeks prior to the first sampling tour to make sure that all supplies are available and all equipment is in working condition. This allows time to make required repairs and order replacement equipment. Inspect the nets, waders, and gloves (if electrofishing) for tears. Ensure water quality meters can be calibrated and are properly functioning as described in SOP #3. Equipment and supplies for field and laboratory use is shown in Table 1.

Table 1. Field equipment and supplies for monitoring fish communities.

| Number Required | Description |
|---|---|
| GENERAL | |
| Per Person | Waders and boots<br>Life jackets<br>Rain Gear<br>Polarized sun glasses<br>First aide kit<br>Insect repellent & sunscreen |
| 1 | First aide kit, insect repellent & sunscreen |
| 1 | Park radio & charger |
| 1 | Directions to sample sites & sample site maps |
| 1 | GPS unit and list of GPS coordinates |
| 1 | Digital camera |
| 1-2 | Clip board with pencils, permanent markers, *etc.* |
| Complete set | Data sheets for habitat and fish community data |
| 1 | Backpack for carrying buckets |
| 1 | Backpack for carrying water quality meters and small equipment |
| Various | Field guides |
| 1 | Stop watch for recording sampling effort |
| Each state and Federal | Collecting permits |
| 1 | Field log book |

Table 1. Field equipment and supplies for monitoring fish communities (continued).

| Number Required | Description |
|---|---|
| 1 | Flagging tape, roll |
| 1 | Tool box with miscellaneous tools including volt/ohm meter |
| 1 | Battery charger for rechargeable batteries |
| 1 | Battery charger for backpack shocker and tow barge batteries |
| Size and number varies by instrument | Extra batteries for hand-held water quality meters, velocity meter, datasondes, weighing balance, range finder |
| **HABITAT ASSESSMENT & WATER QUALITY** | |
| 1 | Tape measure (100 or 50 m) |
| 1 | Range finder |
| 1 | Velocity meter (Marsh-McBirney or USGS pygmy) with copies of operations manuals |
| 1 | Top-setting wading rod, 1.5 m |
| 1 | Laminated plastic substrate sheet with Wentworth scale codes (for electrofished parks only) |
| 1 | YSI 55 hand-held meter and batteries (for use at TAPR only) |
| 1 | YSI 63 hand-held meter and batteries (for use at TAPR only) |
| 1-3 depending on number of reaches sampled | Datasonde for water quality |
| 1 per sonde | Pvc cage, chain, and lock for securing datasonde |
| 1 bottle of each | Calibration solutions: pH 7, pH 10, Conductivity, and Turbidity |
| 1 | Thermometer |
| 1 | Turbidity tube (for use at TAPR only) |
| **FISH SAMPLING** | |
| 2-3 | Minnow seines |
| 1-2 | Backpack electrofishing unit (backpack, cathode, anode, batteries, battery charger) |
| 1 | Tow barge electrofishing unit (barge, generator, battery, pulse box, cathode, anode, gas can with gas, oil) |
| 4-5 | Dip nets |
| 1 pair per person | Electrofishing gloves |
| 4-5 | 5 gal. buckets to hold fish |
| 4-5 | 1 gal. buckets to sort fish |
| 1 | Cooler to hold additional fish |
| 3-4 | Aquarium nets |
| 4-5 | Aerators, battery powered |
| 1 | Measuring board (in mm) |
| 1 | Weighing balance ($\pm$ 1g) and batteries |
| 1 | Shallow pan for placing fish on balance |
| Varies per reach and park | 1 gal. jugs for preserving fish |
| Varies per reach | Jar labels printed on waterproof paper |
| Varies per # of samples | 10% buffered formalin and 1-L plastic Nalgene bottles for carrying, bring extra quantities to ensure enough is available to preserve all samples. |

## II. Field Forms

Print copies of field sheets and labels on waterproof paper. Data should be recorded with waterproof ink or #2 lead pencil. Example data sheets are provided as attachments to their corresponding SOPs. A complete list of all forms and data sheets required is presented in Table 2.

Table 2. List of field forms and data sheets required for fish community monitoring for the sampling season.

| TITLE | PURPOSE | NUMBER OF COPIES NEEDED PER REACH |
|---|---|---|
| **Seined Parks** | | |
| Reach and Weather Conditions Form –Seined Parks | Recording weather and stream conditions | 1 |
| Physical Habitat Form – Seined Parks | Recording in-stream habitat and riparian data | 3-5 depending on number of sites sampled within reach |
| Individual Fish Data Form – Seined Parks | Recording fish collection data | As needed; typically 3-5 |
| **Electrofished Parks** | | |
| In-stream Habitat Assessment Form | Recording in-stream physical habitat data | 1 |
| Fish Cover Form | Recording in-stream and bank cover for fish | 1 |
| Bank Measurement Form | Recording bank stability and vegetation data | 1 |
| Reach and Weather Conditions Form – Electrofished Parks | Recording site and weather data | 1 |
| Individual Fish Data Form – Electrofished Parks | Recording fish collection data | As needed; typically 1-3 per reach |
| Stream Discharge Form | Recording stream discharge | 1 |

## IV. Collecting permits

Collecting permits for sampling fish will be obtained from the appropriate natural resource agency where fish are sampled. For PIPE and TAPR, a collecting permit from the U.S. Fish and Wildlife Service is mandatory for fish collection due to the presence of Topeka shiners. Contact information for permit applications for each state is:

Arkansas Game and Fish Commission, Attn: Scientific Collection Permit, #2 Natural Resources Drive, Little Rock, AR 72205.

Iowa Department of Natural Resources, Customer Service Bureau – Licensing Section, Wallace State Office Building, 502 East 9th Street, Des Moines, IW 50319-0034.

Kansas Department of Wildlife and Parks, Attn: Environmental Services Section, 512 SE 25th Avenue, Pratt, KS 67124

Minnesota Department of Natural Resources, 500 Layfayette Road, St. Paul, MN 55155-4020.

Missouri Department of Conservation, P.O. Box 180, Jefferson City, MO 65102-0180.

Nebraska Game and Parks Commission, 2200 N. 33$^{rd}$ Street, P.O Box 30370, Lincoln, NE 68847-6057.

US Fish and Wildlife Service. Region 3 (Minnesota), phone: 612-713-536, 1 Federal Drive, BHW Federal Building, Fort Snelling, MN 55111, and Region 6 (Kansas), phone: 303-236-7905, 134 Union Blvd., Lakewood, CO 80228.

## Protocol for Monitoring Fish Communities in Small Streams in the Heartland Inventory and Monitoring Network

## SOP 2: Training

## Version 1.00 (05/01/2008)

**Revision History Log:**

| Previous Version # | Revision Date | Author | Changes Made | Reason for Change | New Version # |
|---|---|---|---|---|---|
| | | | | | |
| | | | | | |
| | | | | | |
| | | | | | |
| | | | | | |

This SOP explains the training procedures for using field equipment properly and collecting fish community and habitat data. This training ensures a high level of consistency among crew members. Prior to training, all personnel will review the protocol and each SOP. Someone familiar with the protocol and experience with the sampling procedures should supervise the training.

### I. Field Sampling and Habitat Data Collection

Procedure:

1. All crew members should practice field methods for collecting water quality (SOP #3), fish (SOP #4), habitat (SOP #5) and discharge (SOP #6) data in a nearby stream. The project leader will train the crew to ensure that each person is comfortable with all aspects of the sampling routine and that they are able to use all equipment properly and safely.
2. All personnel also will review photographs, descriptions, and a reference collection of common fish species occurring at each park.

**Protocol for Monitoring Fish Communities in Small Streams in the Heartland Inventory and Monitoring Network**

**SOP 3: Documenting CORE 5 Water Quality Variables**

**Version 1.00 (XX/XX/2008)**

**Revision History Log:**

| Previous Version # | Revision Date | Author | Changes Made | Reason for Change | New Version # |
|---|---|---|---|---|---|
|  |  |  |  |  |  |
|  |  |  |  |  |  |
|  |  |  |  |  |  |
|  |  |  |  |  |  |
|  |  |  |  |  |  |

This SOP addresses the equipment and methods required to measure CORE 5 water quality variables (temperature, dissolved oxygen, specific conductance, pH, and turbidity) in association with all aquatic monitoring in network parks. Detailed guidance for measuring CORE 5 parameters, including training, calibration, QA/QC, data archiving, meter specifications, field measurements, and trouble shooting, can be found in the Documenting CORE 5 Water Quality Variables SOP located at: http://www1.nature.nps.gov/im/units/htln/fish.cfm. This SOP is based on guidance from NPS-WRD (2003), and Wagner *et al*. (2006).

**I. Unattended CORE 5 measurements**

Unattended CORE 5 data will be recorded using dataloggers or sondes. CORE 5 water quality parameters measured at small intervals (*i.e.*, minutes to hours) are considered continuous because few if any significant water quality changes are likely to go unrecorded. When the goal is to characterize events of short duration, but such events are difficult to capture manually using discrete measurements (see below), continuous monitoring is appropriate. Continuous monitoring of core parameters helps address questions concerning daily variability or short-term changes (*e.g.*, precipitation related events) that might not be apparent or may prevent accurate understanding of long-term data. Continuous monitoring also provides the most comprehensive temporal data set to assess variability through time. Such information is necessary to document correlations, possible cause and effect relationships, and differentiate natural variability from anthropogenic induced change to an aquatic system. Because loggers give more comprehensive data and are easily deployed in these small streams, and discrete samples would duplicate effort, we will use loggers to collect water quality data at all parks. Data logging of CORE 5 parameters will be conducted for a minimum of 48 hours at each reach during the sampling period. At TAPR, where reaches far outnumber the availability of sondes, only a select number of reaches will be monitored using these sondes.

## II. Discrete CORE 5 measurements

Discrete CORE 5 measurements using hand-held meters do not reflect changes in water quality, such as diurnal fluctuations or those associated with a hydrologic event. These measurements serve two general purposes: (1) they represent the natural condition of the surface water at the time of sampling, although they are not intended to be a precise measure of water-quality condition in the stream, and (2) they serve as a cross-check for CORE 5 measurements using unattended CORE 5 datasondes (see above). Because it is not feasible to deploy data sondes in every reach at TAPR, discrete measurements are taken at TAPR at each site sampled within each reach during time of fish sampling. All other parks will use only unattended CORE 5 sampling with sondes deployed at each reach.

## III. Analysis and Reporting

CORE 5 data will be analyzed using summary statistics (mean, median, range, standard deviation, standard error) for each reach and date. This information will be presented in summary and synthesis reports to support fish collection data.

## III. NPS STORET

Collected water quality data that has been successfully subjected to QA/QC will be exported to NPS STORET (see SOP #8 Data Management). Only summary data for a site and collection period in addition to pertinent metadata will be submitted. Instructions for preparing and exporting water quality data to this archival facility can be found at the following website:

http://nrdata.nps.gov/Programs/Water/NPStoret/

**Protocol for Monitoring Fish Communities in Small Streams in the Heartland Inventory and Monitoring Network**

**SOP 4: Fish Community Sampling**

**Version 1.00 (05/01/2008)**

**Revision History Log:**

| Previous Version # | Revision Date | Author | Changes Made | Reason for Change | New Version # |
|---|---|---|---|---|---|
|  |  |  |  |  |  |
|  |  |  |  |  |  |
|  |  |  |  |  |  |
|  |  |  |  |  |  |
|  |  |  |  |  |  |

The fish sampling protocols described in this SOP present methods for collecting a representative sample of the fish community from a stream. Such a sample should contain most, if not all, species in the stream at the time of sampling, in numbers proportional to their actual abundance.

For parks previously monitored using seining techniques (HOME, PIPE, TAPR), the methodology presented below follows closely with Peitz and Rowell (2004). Parks added to the long-term monitoring program (EFMO, HEHO, HOSP, GWCA, PERI, WICR) where electrofishing methods will be used follow guidance in Petersen *et al.* (2008). The methods have been modified from these two protocols, where appropriate, to meet the specific objectives of monitoring fish in small streams. Modifications to Peitz and Rowell (2004) have been made to enhance data collection without compromising comparisons to historical data collected under the original protocol. Further, only those portions of the Petersen *et al.* (2008) protocol applicable to electrofishing in small wadeable streams are included here. This SOP presents techniques for fish sampling and procedures for processing fish.

**I. Reach, Weather, and Sampling Conditions**

Procedures:

1. Record the four letter park code, stream name and/or stream number, reach (for electrofished parks the reach *will always* be called 'lower'), date, reach length (for electrofished parks), and reach description on the Reach and Weather Conditions forms.

2. Record weather conditions and reach conditions (for seined parks) and note any other weather or reach conditions that might affect sampling efficiency.

3. During initial establishment of the permanent reach, upper and lower boundaries will be documented using a GPS unit. Proper use of GPS units for collecting location data can be found at the following website: *http://www1.nature.nps.gov/im/units/htln/data_management/data_management.htm* This should be done only on the first visit to a stream, for all electrofished streams. Because three to five sites/locations are sampled within the permanent reaches at PIPE, TAPR, and HOME, GPS coordinates will be collected at each site sampled within the reach each year.

## II. Seining Methods for Wadeable Streams (PIPE, TAPR, and HOME)

Wadeable streams can be sampled using a "common sense" seine (1.2 m tall with a 6.44 mm mesh size) or a bag seine, depending on the size of the stream. Use and effectiveness of a particular seine depends on the channel units (e.g., riffles, runs, pools), channel size, and instream habitat/structure present in the sampling reach. Seines are most commonly used in wadeable streams with smaller substrates such as gravel or sand with little or no woody debris. The presence of submerged objects such as woody snags or boulders in a sampling area can make it difficult to collect a representative sample. Therefore, the potential for collecting a representative and repeatable sample should be evaluated before seining an area. For sampling riffles, which typically have larger gravel and cobble substrate, a method known as kick seining is used. Seining methods, which are less invasive than other techniques, were selected for PIPE and TAPR due to the presence of the federally endangered Topeka shiner. At HOME, the soft bottom and turbid conditions at Cub Creek makes seining methods ideal for sampling fish.

## Selecting Sample Sites within a Reach:

1. An attempt should be made to sample fish from five sites (or locations) within each reach (see Figure 1). Previous monitoring under the prairie fish protocol suggests that not all stream reaches contain enough water to sample five sites. Therefore, three to five sample sites will represent the stream reaches sampled. If water levels are too low to obtain samples from at least three sites, that reach will not be sampled.

2. Sample sites should be chosen based on availability of channel units (riffles, runs, pools) within the reach. Pools are the predominant channel unit in prairie streams, and accordingly, most samples will be taken from this habitat.

3. Within the reach, sampling always starts with the most downstream site and moves upstream to avoid fouling water at upstream sites prior to sampling (Figure 1).

4. The channel unit type for each site should be recorded on the habitat data sheets (see SOP #5) and all fish collected at a site are kept separate for recording purposes (see Sample Processing section below).

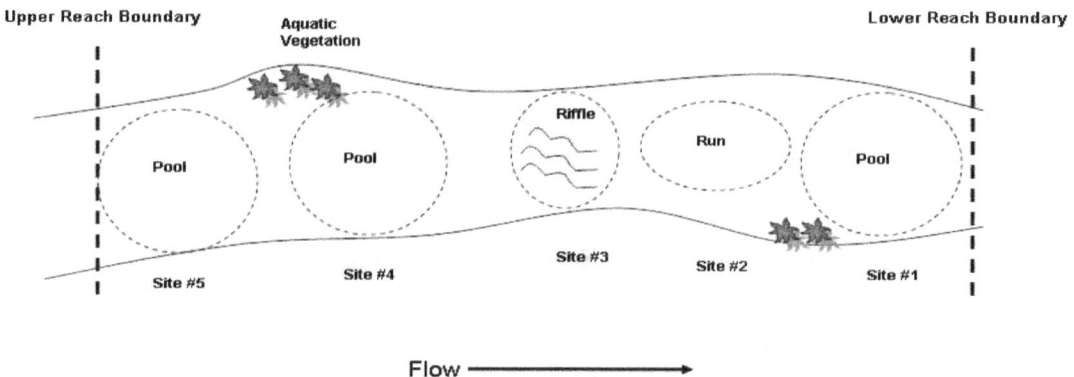

Figure 1. Hypothetical reach and site placement for streams sampled with seining methods.

**Seining Techniques:**

1. Fish are captured using a two man common sense seine with an approximate height of 1.2 m and a mesh size of 6.44 mm. Width of seine used will vary depending on width of stream.

2. Within a site, sampling is conducted with the direction of flow.

3. Sampling Pool and Run Channel Units: Two crew members conducting the sampling enter the site at the upstream end. The seine is extended the full width of channel, if possible. One or two (depending on site width) crew members hold a second seine at the bottom of the site to block fish from moving downstream and out of the site. See Figure 2.

   a. Seine is hauled in a downstream direction with the lead line held on the stream bottom.
   b. Seining speed is slightly faster than the current allowing for fish to be trapped against the net. Faster speeds will push water in front of the seine and force fish away from the net.
   c. When crew members reach the block net, they should swoop one end of the seine in front of the block net and onto the bank. At the same time, those holding the block net should raise their net out of the water, collecting fish that avoided the seine.

4. Sampling Riffle Channel Units: Kick seining involves shortening the length of a common sense seine by rolling the seine onto the brails. The seine is then placed at the downstream end of the riffle by one or two crewmembers, and the substrate is kicked to dislodge benthic fish species that are carried by the current into the seine. See Figure 2.

5. All captured fish are immediately placed in aerated buckets, containing water taken from the site. All fish from a site are processed separately.

Figure 2. Example of seining pools/runs (left) and kick seining riffles (right).

## III. Electrofishing Methods for Wadeable Streams (EFMO, GWCA, HEHO, HOSP, PERI, and WICR)

Electrofishing is the use of electricity to capture fish. A high-voltage potential is applied between two or more electrodes that are placed in the water. The voltage potential is created with either direct current or alternating current; only direct current will be used in this protocol due to lower incidence of injury to fish. Direct current produces a unidirectional, constant electrical current. Pulsed direct current, a modified direct current, produces a unidirectional electrical current composed of a sequence of cyclic impulses (Meador *et al.*, 1993). The frequency of the pulses produced when using pulsed direct current can be adjusted by the operator.

**General Electrofishing Procedures:**

1. Channel width, depth, and access should be considered before choosing between backpack and tow barge electrofishing methods (Figure 3).

   a. Backpack electrofishing (with a single anode) should be used in shallow (<1 m) and narrow (<5 m wide) reaches. A crew of three is needed.
   b. Towed electrofishing gear (multiple anodes) is more effective in wide (>5 m) wadeable reaches with pools deeper than 1 m. A crew of 5 is needed.

2. All crewmembers must wear low voltage rubber gloves and waders to protect them from the electrical current and wear polarized glasses to enhance their ability to see fish.

3. Techniques for set up and collecting samples using either backpack or towed electrofishing gear are generally similar.

Figure 3. Backpack (left) and tow barge (right) electrofishing gear used in wadeable streams.

**Procedures for Setting Electrofishing Gear:**

1. Prior to sampling, measure conductivity of the water to aid in selecting voltage, frequency, and duty cycle for the electrofishing gear being used. Note: Effectiveness of electrofishing gear is primarily affected by water conductivity.

   a. Low conductivity water is resistant to flow, reducing the amount of electrical current traveling through the water.
   b. High conductivity water concentrates a narrow electrical field between the electrodes (Meador *et al.,* 1993).

2. General Rule for Voltage: output of electrofishing gear should be ~ 3,000 watts. Voltage times amperage equals wattage. If the gear is without ammeters, some pre-sampling experimentation is necessary.

   a. In low conductivity water, high voltage and low amperage are needed.
   b. In high conductivity water, low voltage and high amperage are needed.

3. General Rule for Frequency: a pulse rate range from 30 to 60 pulses per second (pps) should be used. Frequencies >60 pulses per second (pps) are effective in collecting fish but can cause injuries, especially to larger fish (Coffelt Manufacturing, Inc., cited in Meador *et al,.* 1993; McMichael *et al.,* 1998). Pulse rates <30 pps have caused low incidence of injury, but are generally ineffective in collecting fish. Therefore, pulse rate should be set to

produce an effective collection of all fish species and sizes while minimizing injury.

4. General Rule for Duty Cycle: a range of 25% - 100% should be used. Duty cycle is calculated as: pulse frequency X pulse duration X 100. Electrofishing with intermediate to high duty cycles reduces injury and mortality to fish (Dolan and Miranda, 2004).

**Sampling Direction:**

1. Regardless of the gear used, a single electrofishing pass is made in the reach (Figure 4).

2. Sampling begins at the downstream boundary of the sampling reach and proceeds upstream. Sampling in an upstream direction in wadeable streams is preferred because disturbance of the streambed by crewmembers increases turbidity and reduces visibility of the stunned fish (Hendricks *et al.*, 1980).

Sampling requires alternating between banks in a "zigzag" pattern to cover habitat features as one proceeds upstream (Figure 4). Using the zigzag pattern, every effort is made to sample all geomorphic channel units (riffles, runs, pools) and instream habitat features, such as woody snags, undercut banks, macrophyte beds, or large boulders.

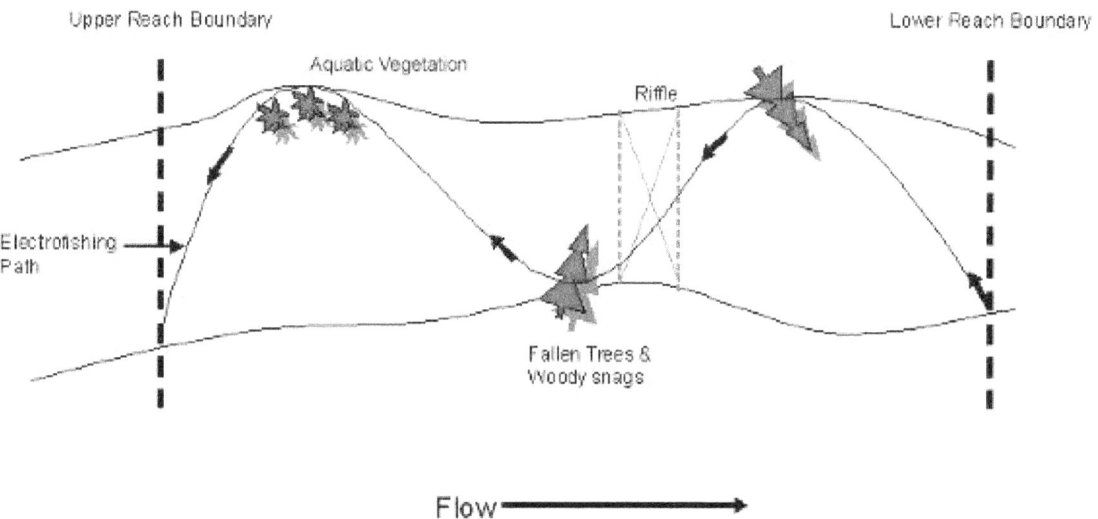

Figure 4. Single pass zigzag sampling technique used in backpack or towed electrofishing for wadeable streams.

**Electrofishing Techniques:**

1. Continuous application of electrical current and herding of fish by the operator is used in open run habitats. Fish generally respond to continuous electrical current by avoiding exposure to the electrical field, resulting in fish moving just ahead and away from the operator. The operator uses the current to herd the fish into natural barriers such as banks, bars, or shallow riffles to facilitate capture.

2. Intermittent application of electrical current and herding fish to the operator can be used in runs or long pools in *narrow* reaches. This technique requires a crewmember (or two) to enter the reach upstream of the operator. The crewmember(s) moves downstream toward the operator, creating a disturbance and driving fish downstream. The electricity is turned on once the fish are visible and close to the anode.

3. To sample shallow riffles, the operator sweeps the anode across the riffle from upstream to downstream while walking across the riffle. Crewmembers with nets are positioned downstream of the operator to collect stunned fish.

4. The ambush technique should be used when a reach has complex instream habitat such as woody debris, boulder fields, etc. Using this technique, the operator approaches the habitat feature with the electrical current off. In quick succession, the anode is thrust close to the habitat feature, the current is turned on, and the anode is withdrawn from the feature. This produces galvanotaxis, where the current forces the fish to swim out from the habitat feature and towards the anode (Meador *et al.*, 1993).

## IV. Sample Processing

The goal of processing fish in the field is to collect information on taxonomic identification, length, weight, abundance, and the presence of external anomalies, with minimal harm to specimens that will be released alive back into the stream. Many species are too small or difficult to identify in the field. These specimens must be brought back to the laboratory for processing. All threatened and endangered species or candidate species for listing will be released where they were collected.

Procedures:

1. Captured fish are placed in a live cage or aerated holding tanks during processing to reduce stress and mortality. Regardless of the effort made to minimize handling and stress to fish, some mortality will occur.

2. Sort fish into identifiable and unidentifiable groups. Identifications are made to species level by a crewmember that is familiar with the fish species commonly found in the study area. Taxonomic nomenclature follows that established by the

American Fisheries Society's Committee on Names of Fishes (Robins *et al*., 1991). Always process threatened and endangered or sensitive fish species before other identifiable species.

3. Obtain a subsample of 30 individuals per species from a reach to measure. A "blind grab" technique is used where a dip net is passed through the entire bucket or holding tank to ensure fish of various sizes are captured with each "grab".

    a. For reaches in which fish are seined (PIPE, TAPR, and HOME), all fish collected from a site will be kept separate during processing and recording. Fish of a particular species will continue to be measured at all sites until 30 individuals have been measured for the reach.

        i. For example, 20 bluntnose minnows are collected at site #1, 13 collected from site #2, and 6 collected from site #3. The 20 fish from site #1 would be measured and recorded on the site #1 data sheet and 10 fish from site #2 would be measured and recorded on site #2 data sheet. Now that 30 have been measured for the reach, the remaining bluntnose minnows from sites #2 and #3 would be counted and recorded under their respective data sheets.

4. Measure total length (Figure 5) and weight of 30 individuals for each species and record any anomalies.

    a. Length measurements are determined by using a measuring board consisting of a linear metric scale on a flat wooden or plastic base with a stop at the zero point. Total length is taken from tip of snout (with mouth closed) to end of caudal fin (while depressed). See Figure 5.

    b. Weight measurements are obtained by using portable electronic scales (Figure 5).

    c. A batch weight will be recorded for smaller species (*e.g.*, minnows, darters, sculpins, and madtoms). Individual weights will be recorded for species that have a large size range (*e.g.*, bass, sunfish, catfish, suckers).

    d. Record anomalies and presence of black spot (*Neascus* spp.), a fish parasite, for each fish measured. Anomalies are externally visible skin or subcutaneous disorders or parasites (Ohio EPA, 1987). They include deformities, eroded fins, lesions, and tumors, collectively referred to as "DELT anomalies" (Sanders *et al*., 1999). Other external anomalies, such as anchor worm (*Lernaea* spp.) and popeye disease, should also be noted in the comments section next to the measurements for an individual fish.

    e. Once 30 fish of a species have been measured from a reach, the remaining specimens are counted.

Figure 5. Total length measurement for an individual (left) and batch weight for a subsample of smaller fish (right).

6. Record data on the Individual Fish Data form.

    a. Record the park code, stream name and/or stream number, reach (for electrofished reaches record "lower"), date, gear used, and sampling effort (time spent seining or electrofishing).

    b. For streams sampled with a seine, record the site number and make certain that **fish from different sites within a reach are recorded on separate data sheets**. Also record the time at which each site was seined.

    c. For streams that are sampled with electrofishing gear, record the three letter initials of all crewmembers. Record the person identifying/measuring fish, the person recording the data, and those who operated the electrofishing equipment and netted fish.

    d. For each individual of a species, record the length and any anomalies. For larger fish, record individual weights. For smaller fish, batch weigh 30 specimens (Figure 5). Any Topeka shiners collected should be aged (immature or mature), if possible.

    e. Record the additional number of fish collected for each species under "Species Count". For example, if 46 white suckers were collected at a reach, 30 fish would be measured and weighed and the remaining 16 would be counted (*i.e.*, Species Count = 16).

7. Preserve selected specimens (i.e., those too small or difficult to identify in the field) in 10 percent buffered formalin for later identification in the laboratory or for a reference collection.

    a. Make a small incision along the body of specimens larger than 100 mm. This allows formalin to penetrate the body cavity.

b.  All unidentified specimens collected within a reach using electrofishing gear can be preserved in a single jar with a label that contains the park, stream name and/or number, reach, date, gear type, and sampling effort. For seined reaches, unknown specimens from each site within the reach should be preserved in separate jars and the site number should also be recorded on the label.

c.  All preserved specimens will be identified at the HTLN Aquatic Program laboratory at Missouri State University using a microscope and relevant identification keys and field guides (Smith, 1979; Robinson and Buchanan, 1988; Cross and Collins, 1995; Pflieger, 1997; Bosanko, 2007). Specimens not used for a reference collection will be disposed of after one year.

# REACH AND WEATHER CONDITIONS FORM – SEINED PARKS

**Park:** _____  **Stream No.:** _____  **Stream Reach :** _____

**Date:** _____  **Time:** _____  **State:** _____  **County:** _____

**Drainage Basin:** _____  **Locality:** _____

**Collectors:** _____ (three letter initials)

**Weather** (circle):   clear-sunny   partly cloudy   cloudy   raining   other:_____
_____

**In stream flow for stream reach** (circle):   isolated pools   trickle between pools   flow between pools

**Off-channel pools for stream reach** (circle):   present   absent   not applicable (Isolated pool / Spring)

**Spring present in stream reach** (circle): Yes  No   **Pictures of reach taken?** (circle): Yes  No

General Comments (aquatic vegetation, stream bed stability, sampling effectiveness, upstream land use, mortality, disease,
etc.):_____
_____
_____
_____
_____
_____
_____
_____
_____

# INDIVIDUAL FISH DATA FORM – SEINED PARKS

Park: _____  Stream #: _____  Stream Reach): _____  Site #:_____

Date: _____  Time: _____  Gear: _____  Effort (sec.) _____

Anomalies: D = deformities, E = eroded fins, L = Lesions, T = tumors, B = blackspot
Age = Juvenile (J) or Mature (M)    Vchrd = Vouchered (yes/no)    Cmts = Comments

| Species: | | | | | |
|---|---|---|---|---|---|
| TL (mm) | Wt (g) | Anom | Age | Vchrd | Cmts |
| | | | | | |
| | | | | | |
| | | | | | |
| | | | | | |
| | | | | | |
| | | | | | |
| | | | | | |
| | | | | | |
| | | | | | |
| | | | | | |
| | | | | Species Count: | |

| Species: | | | | | |
|---|---|---|---|---|---|
| TL (mm) | Wt (g) | Anom | Age | Vchrd | Cmts |
| | | | | | |
| | | | | | |
| | | | | | |
| | | | | | |
| | | | | | |
| | | | | | |
| | | | | | |
| | | | | | |
| | | | | | |
| | | | | | |
| | | | | Species Count: | |

| Species: | | | | | |
|---|---|---|---|---|---|
| TL (mm) | Wt (g) | Anom | Age | Vchrd | Cmts |
| | | | | | |
| | | | | | |
| | | | | | |
| | | | | | |
| | | | | | |
| | | | | | |
| | | | | | |
| | | | | | |
| | | | | | |
| | | | | | |
| | | | | Species Count: | |

| Species: | | | | | |
|---|---|---|---|---|---|
| TL (mm) | Wt (g) | Anom | Age | Vchrd | Cmts |
| | | | | | |
| | | | | | |
| | | | | | |
| | | | | | |
| | | | | | |
| | | | | | |
| | | | | | |
| | | | | | |
| | | | | | |
| | | | | | |
| | | | | Species Count: | |

| Species: | | | | | |
|---|---|---|---|---|---|
| TL (mm) | Wt (g) | Anom | Age | Vchrd | Cmts |
| | | | | | |
| | | | | | |
| | | | | | |
| | | | | | |
| | | | | | |
| | | | | | |
| | | | | | |
| | | | | | |
| | | | | | |
| | | | | | |
| | | | | Species Count: | |

| Species: | | | | | |
|---|---|---|---|---|---|
| TL (mm) | Wt (g) | Anom | Age | Vchrd | Cmts |
| | | | | | |
| | | | | | |
| | | | | | |
| | | | | | |
| | | | | | |
| | | | | | |
| | | | | | |
| | | | | | |
| | | | | | |
| | | | | | |
| | | | | Species Count: | |

# REACH AND WEATHER CONDITIONS FORM – ELECTROFISHED PARKS

Park:_____  Stream Name:_____  Stream #:_____  Reach: _____

Reach Length(m):_____  Date:_____  Recorder:_____

Reach Description:_____

_____

_____

_____

**Weather Conditions:**

Cloud cover:_____%      Wind*:  Calm    Light    Moderate    Gusty*

Precipitation: *None    Rain    Sleet    Snow*      Intensity: *N/A    Light    Moderate    Heavy*

Other Weather:_____

Additional Comments:_____

_____

_____

_____

_____

_____

# INDIVIDUAL FISH DATA – ELECTROFISHED PARKS

page ____ of ____

Park: _____  Stream Name: _____  Stream#: _____  Reach: _____

Date: _____  IDed by: _____  Recorder: _____  Gear: _____  Effort (sec.): _____

Crew: *Shocker(s):* _____  *Barge:* _____  *Netter(s):* _____

## Anomalies: D = deformities, E = eroded fins, L = Lesions, T = tumors, B = Blackspot

| Species: | | | | |
|---|---|---|---|---|
| TL (mm) | Wt (g) | Anom | Vchrd | Cmts |
| | | | | |
| | | | | |
| | | | | |
| | | | | |
| | | | | |
| | | | | |
| | | | | |
| | | | | |
| | | | | |
| | | | | |
| | | *Species Count:* | | |

| Species: | | | | |
|---|---|---|---|---|
| TL (mm) | Wt (g) | Anom | Vchrd | Cmts |
| | | | | |
| | | | | |
| | | | | |
| | | | | |
| | | | | |
| | | | | |
| | | | | |
| | | | | |
| | | | | |
| | | | | |
| | | *Species Count:* | | |

| Species: | | | | |
|---|---|---|---|---|
| TL (mm) | Wt (g) | Anom | Vchrd | Cmts |
| | | | | |
| | | | | |
| | | | | |
| | | | | |
| | | | | |
| | | | | |
| | | | | |
| | | | | |
| | | | | |
| | | | | |
| | | *Species Count:* | | |

| Species: | | | | |
|---|---|---|---|---|
| TL (mm) | Wt (g) | Anom | Vchrd | Cmts |
| | | | | |
| | | | | |
| | | | | |
| | | | | |
| | | | | |
| | | | | |
| | | | | |
| | | | | |
| | | | | |
| | | | | |
| | | *Species Count:* | | |

| Species: | | | | |
|---|---|---|---|---|
| TL (mm) | Wt (g) | Anom | Vchrd | Cmts |
| | | | | |
| | | | | |
| | | | | |
| | | | | |
| | | | | |
| | | | | |
| | | | | |
| | | | | |
| | | | | |
| | | | | |
| | | *Species Count:* | | |

| Species: | | | | |
|---|---|---|---|---|
| TL (mm) | Wt (g) | Anom | Vchrd | Cmts |
| | | | | |
| | | | | |
| | | | | |
| | | | | |
| | | | | |
| | | | | |
| | | | | |
| | | | | |
| | | | | |
| | | | | |
| | | *Species Count:* | | |

| Species: | | | | |
|---|---|---|---|---|
| TL (mm) | Wt (g) | Anom | Vchrd | Cmts |
| | | | | |
| | | | | |
| | | | | |
| | | | | |
| | | | | |
| | | | | |
| | | | | |
| | | | | |
| | | | | |
| | | | | |
| | | *Species Count:* | | |

| Species: | | | | |
|---|---|---|---|---|
| TL (mm) | Wt (g) | Anom | Vchrd | Cmts |
| | | | | |
| | | | | |
| | | | | |
| | | | | |
| | | | | |
| | | | | |
| | | | | |
| | | | | |
| | | | | |
| | | | | |
| | | *Species Count:* | | |

| Species: | | | | |
|---|---|---|---|---|
| TL (mm) | Wt (g) | Anom | Vchrd | Cmts |
| | | | | |
| | | | | |
| | | | | |
| | | | | |
| | | | | |
| | | | | |
| | | | | |
| | | | | |
| | | | | |
| | | | | |
| | | *Species Count:* | | |

| Species: | | | | |
|---|---|---|---|---|
| TL (mm) | Wt (g) | Anom | Vchrd | Cmts |
| | | | | |
| | | | | |
| | | | | |
| | | | | |
| | | | | |
| | | | | |
| | | | | |
| | | | | |
| | | | | |
| | | | | |
| | | *Species Count:* | | |

| Species: | | | | |
|---|---|---|---|---|
| TL (mm) | Wt (g) | Anom | Vchrd | Cmts |
| | | | | |
| | | | | |
| | | | | |
| | | | | |
| | | | | |
| | | | | |
| | | | | |
| | | | | |
| | | | | |
| | | | | |
| | | *Species Count:* | | |

| Species: | | | | |
|---|---|---|---|---|
| TL (mm) | Wt (g) | Anom | Vchrd | Cmts |
| | | | | |
| | | | | |
| | | | | |
| | | | | |
| | | | | |
| | | | | |
| | | | | |
| | | | | |
| | | | | |
| | | | | |
| | | *Species Count:* | | |

Jar Labels for Seined Parks

Jar Labels for Electrofished Parks

| Park: |
| Stream Name or #: |
| Reach:               Date: |
| Site #:              Site type: |
| Gear: |
| Effort (sec.): |

| Park: |
| Stream Name or #: |
| Reach:               Date: |
| Site #:              Site type: |
| Gear: |
| Effort (sec.): |

| Park: |
| Stream Name or #: |
| Reach:               Date: |
| Site #:              Site type: |
| Gear: |
| Effort (sec.): |

| Park: |
| Stream Name or #: |
| Reach:               Date: |
| Site #:              Site type: |
| Gear: |
| Effort (sec.): |

| Park: |
| Stream Name: |
| Stream #: |
| Reach:               Date: |
| Gear: |
| Effort (sec.): |

| Park: |
| Stream Name: |
| Stream #: |
| Reach:               Date: |
| Gear: |
| Effort (sec.): |

| Park: |
| Stream Name: |
| Stream #: |
| Reach:               Date: |
| Gear: |
| Effort (sec.): |

| Park: |
| Stream Name: |
| Stream #: |
| Reach:               Date: |
| Gear: |
| Effort (sec.): |

**Protocol for Monitoring Fish Communities in Small Streams in the Heartland Inventory and Monitoring Network**

**SOP 5: Physical Habitat Measurements**

**Version 1.00 (05/01/2008)**

**Revision History Log:**

| Previous Version # | Revision Date | Author | Changes Made | Reason for Change | New Version # |
|---|---|---|---|---|---|
|  |  |  |  |  |  |
|  |  |  |  |  |  |
|  |  |  |  |  |  |
|  |  |  |  |  |  |
|  |  |  |  |  |  |

Habitat composition within a stream is an important component in shaping biotic communities. The type and abundance of specific habitat characteristics (*i.e.*, woody debris, substrate size, *etc.*) will influence species presence and relative abundance, as well as size structure of the populations. Because of its importance to fish, physical habitat data will be collected as part of this protocol to examine relationships between environmental conditions and biotic communities. For parks that were previously monitored using seining techniques, methodology presented below follows closely with Peitz and Rowell (2004). Habitat data collected in parks added to the long-term monitoring program (those using electrofishing techniques) will follow Petersen *et al.* (2008). Modifications from the original prairie fish protocol (Peitz and Rowell 2004) have been made to enhance data collection without compromising comparisons to historical data collected under this protocol.

**I. General Procedures**

1. Prior to collecting samples and taking habitat measurements, always complete data sheet information for park code, stream name and/or stream number, reach, date, and time.

2. For electrofished reaches, also record the reach length, transect spacing, and initials of personnel who collect the data.

3. A crew of two to three persons will collect physical habitat data.

4. Equipment necessary to complete habitat sampling is found in SOP #1 (Preparation for Field Sampling).

5. When collecting data, stream banks are referred to in a downstream perspective. Therefore, if the crew is working/collecting data in an upstream direction, river right is on the workers' left, and river left is on the right.

6. Habitat should be collected in conjunction with fish sampling. Data will typically be collected immediately after fish sampling at a reach. If fish sampling takes the entire day to complete, habitat measurements can be collected in the following day or two.

## II. Collecting Habitat Data in Seined Reaches

1. Habitat sampling is conducted only at sites sampled within the reach. In other words, locations within the reach that are not seined will not have habitat data collected. Habitat is collected at three transects per site sampled (Figure 1). They are placed at the upstream and downstream end and in the center of each site. Measurements are recorded at the center of each transect.

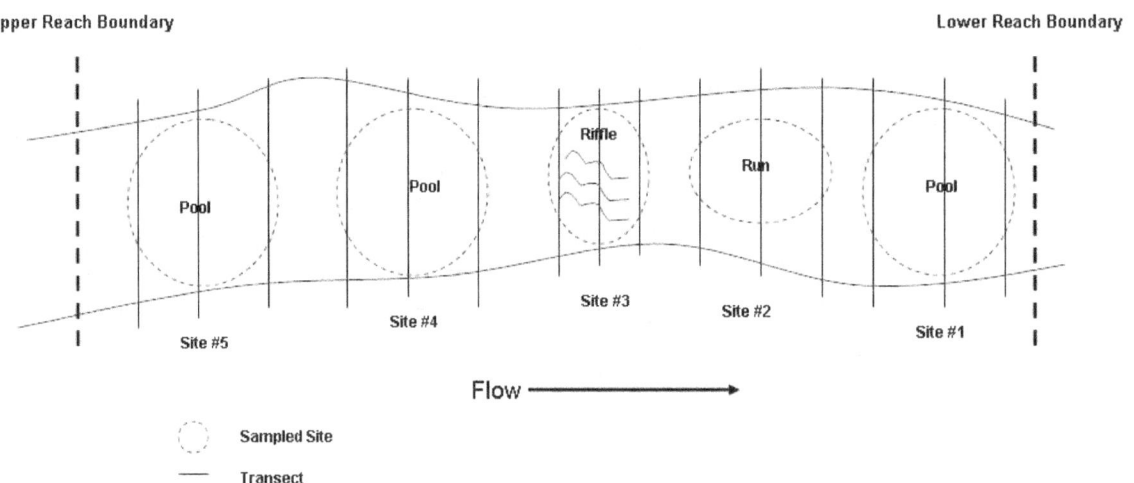

Figure 1. Placement of transects within sample sites of a seined reach.

2. **Measured Parameters**. Record the site type (*i.e.*, channel unit) for each site.

   a. At TAPR, hand-held water quality meters and turbidity tubes are used to collect CORE 5 data, which is recorded on the Physical Habitat Form. This is to be done prior to fish collection and other habitat measurements. Data loggers will be used at specific reach locations at TAPR with the discretion of the project manager.

   b. Data loggers will be used at PIPE and HOME to record water quality data. See SOP #3 for details on CORE 5 data collection.

3. **Site Dimensions**. Measure the length of each site. At each transect measure wetted stream width with a tape measure. At the center of each transect, measure depth and velocity with a velocity meter and wading rod. See SOP #6 for details on collecting depth and velocity using a meter and wading rod.

4. **Site Substrate**. Percent coverage of substrate types are visually estimated from the entire site, not just along the transect.

   a. Record the Daubenmire cover class for each substrate type (Daubenmire, 1959). See Table 1 for description of substrates. The cover classes are: 0 (none present), 1 (0-1%), 2 (1-5%), 3 (5-25%), 4 (25-50%), 5(50-75%), 6 (75-95%), 7 (95-100%).
   b. Record the site stability based on substrate composition. Sites with larger substrates (high amounts of cobble, boulder or bedrock) are stable. Sites with finer substrate (high amounts of muck, silt, or sand) are unstable.

Table 1. Substrate types, size ranges and description.

| Substrate Type | Size Range (mm) | Description |
| --- | --- | --- |
| Muck | <0.004 | Fine material, remains together when squeezed between fingers – not gritty between fingers |
| Detritus | | Fine decayed organic material, original form not distinguishable |
| Silt | 0.004 to 0.06 | Fine material, falls in pieces when squeezed between fingers – not gritty between fingers |
| Sand | 0.06 to 2.0 | Smaller than ladybug size, but visible as particles – gritty between fingers |
| Pea-gravel | 2.0 to 16.0 | Lady bug to marble size |
| Coarse-gravel | 16.0 to 64.0 | Marble to tennis ball size |
| Cobble | 64.0 to 256.0 | Tennis ball to basketball size |
| Boulders | 256.0 to 4000.0 | Basketball to car size |
| Bedrock | > 4000 | Rock bigger than a car |
| Hardpan/shale | | Firm, consolidated fine substrate or shale |

5. **Streambank Erosion**. Estimate the percentage of eroded banks (along entire site) using Daubenmire percentage classes. Highly eroded banks are typically vertical and lack vegetation. Stable banks have a gentle slope (<45° angle) and native vegetation (such as prairie grasses, shrubs, or mature trees). Banks with manicured grasses (lawn) or domestic grasses have less stability than those with native grasses.

6. **Riparian Cover**. Indicate the dominant vegetation along the right and left riparian area of the entire site. Dominant vegetation is identified for distances of 0–25 m, >25–50 m, >50–75 m, >75– 00 m, and >100 m. Vegetation types are described in Table 2.

7. **GPS**. Indicate if the location of each site was recorded using a GPS unit. Proper use of a GPS unit can be found at: *http://www1.nature.nps.gov/im/units/htln/data_management/data_management.ht m*.

Table 2. Codes used to identify dominant riparian vegetation cover classes.

| Vegetation | Code | Description |
|---|---|---|
| Mature woodland | 1 | Large trees present, few mid-story trees or shrubs |
| Woody shrubs / saplings | 2 | Small to midsize trees, early succession trees and shrubs present. Area typical of one disturbed in the recent past |
| Wetland / native grasses & forbs (prairie) | 3 | Native or restored wetland or prairie. Diverse collections of native plants present |
| Domestic grass pasture / hay field | 4 | Dominated by one or two domesticated grasses. Grazed by livestock or hayed |
| Park / lawn | 5 | Frequently mowed or maintained vegetation |
| Row crops | 6 | Area under agricultural crop production |
| Road / railroad | 7 | Dominated by road or railroad bed, vegetation absent |
| Urban / industrial | 8 | Housing or industrial operations present, vegetation absent |
| Other | 9 | Any vegetation type or land use not defined above |

## III. Collecting Habitat Data in Electrofished Reaches

Habitat data is collected at 11 equally spaced transects perpendicular to flow (Figure 2)

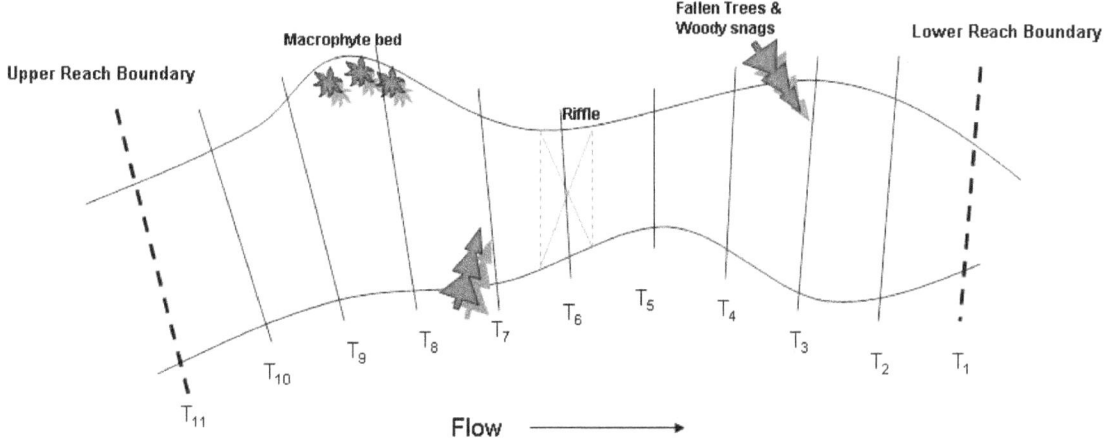

Figure 2. Transect spacing and location within a sample reach.

**Instream Point Habitat Data:**

1. In-stream habitat is collected at three points along each transect: center channel (or middle) and half the distance between center and the left and right banks (Figure 3).

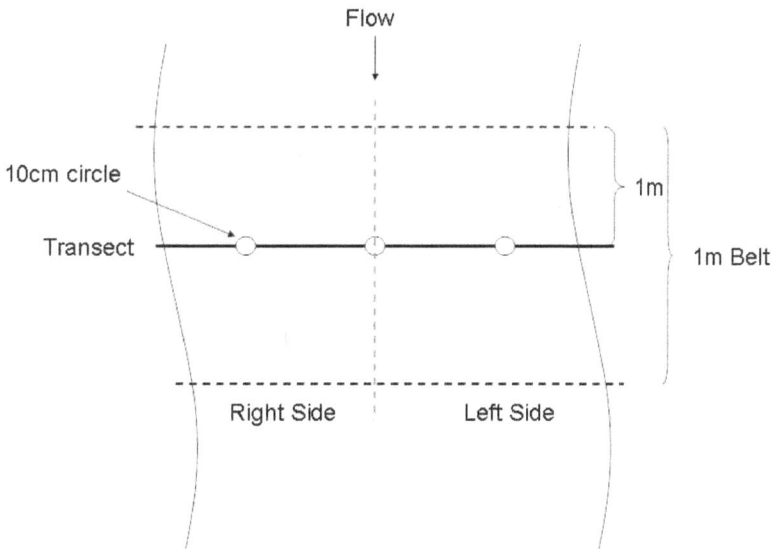

Figure 3. Location of in-stream habitat and fish cover collection at a transect.

2. At each transect, measure wetted width and record channel unit and pool form (if applicable). Channel unit definitions are as follows:

a. <u>Riffle</u>. An area of the stream with steepest slope and shallowest depth, often rocky substrate, and a swift moving current. Thalweg is usually poorly defined.

b. <u>Run or Race</u>. Differ from riffles in that depth of flow is typically greater and slope of the bed is less than that of riffles. Runs will often have a well defined thalweg.

c. <u>Glide</u>. Normally located immediately downstream of pools. The slope of the channel bed through a glide is negative while the slope of the water surface is positive. The head of the glide can be difficult to identify. Use the following characteristics to help you locate the head of the glide:

   1) a location of increased flow velocity coming out of the pool,
   2) a location with a steeply sloped bed rising out of the pool and decreasing to a lesser gradient,
   3) a location where the thalweg coming out of the pool becomes less well defined and essentially fades completely,
   4) a location approximately the same elevation as the tail of the run.

d. <u>Pool</u>. Has a relatively slow current and is usually found at stream channel bends, upstream of riffles, or on the downstream side of obstructions such as boulders or fallen trees. The stream bottom in a pool is often bowl shaped and represents the deepest locations of the reach. Water surface slope of pools at below bankfull flows is near zero.

3. Velocity (meters/second) and depth (centimeters) are measured concurrently at each sample point. Measurements are done using a FLO-MATE Model 2000 or USGS Pygmy current meter attached to a top-setting wading rod. The rod allows for quick and easy measurements of depth with incremental markings and an adjustable arm that places the current meter at the proper depth for measuring velocity (60% of the depth from the surface of the water). Greater detail regarding use of a velocity meter is provided in SOP #6 (Measuring Stream Discharge).

4. Dominant substrate is visually assessed in a 10 cm circle around each point (see Figure 2). Dominant substrate is the average size substrate within the circle based on the Wentworth scale (Table 3; also see Wentworth field sheet at the end of this SOP). For substrate codes 1-3, there are no boxes shown on the field sheet to estimate their respective sizes because these substrates are so small. For these three substrate codes, it is necessary to grab a sample from the plot for assessment. The general rule is:

   a. Code 1 (silt/clay) feels slick between thumb and finger with no evidence of grit.

   b. Code 2 (very fine sand) has a barely perceptible gritty feel.

c.  Code 3 (fine sand) has a distinct gritty texture.

5.  Embeddedness is visually assessed within a 10 cm circle at each point using percentage categories: 0= none (0%), 1= sparse (<10%), 2= moderate (10-40%), 3= heavy (40-75%), 4= very heavy (>75).

6.  Canopy cover is visually observed by looking directly overhead at each point and categorizing the percentage cover within one meter upstream and downstream of a transect. The same categories used for embeddedness are also used for canopy cover. If a bridge or other manmade structure is producing the canopy, record this in the comments section.

Table 3. Substrate size classes to be used for characterizing substrate based on the Wentworth Scale. (Wentworth, 1922)

| Size Code | Particle Diameter Range (mm) | Category |
|---|---|---|
| 1 | <0.062 | Silt/clay |
| 2 | 0.062-0.125 | Very fine sand |
| 3 | 0.125-0.25 | Fine sand |
| 4 | 0.25-0.50 | Medium sand |
| 5 | 0.50-1 | Course sand |
| 6 | 1-2 | Coarse sand |
| 7 | 2-4 | Fine gravel |
| 8 | 4-5.7 | Medium gravel |
| 9 | 5.7-8 | Medium gravel |
| 10 | 8-11.3 | Coarse gravel |
| 11 | 11.3-16 | Coarse gravel |
| 12 | 16-22.6 | Small pebble |
| 13 | 22.6-32 | Small pebble |
| 14 | 32-45 | Large pebble |
| 15 | 45-64 | Large pebble |
| 16 | 64-90 | Small cobble |
| 17 | 90-128 | Small cobble |
| 18 | 128-180 | Large cobble |
| 19 | 180-256 | Large cobble |
| 20 | 256-362 | Boulder |
| 21 | 362-512 | Boulder |
| 22 | 512-1024 | Boulder |
| 23 | >1024 | Boulder |
| 24 | Bedrock | Bedrock |

**Fish Cover:**

1. Assess fish cover by recording all cover types present along each transect. Filamentous algae, hydrophytes, boulders (sizes 21 to 23 on the Wentworth substrate sheet), and any artificial cover are assessed within 10 cm circle around each point. If artificial cover (*e.g.*, cinder block, car tire, *etc.*) is present, the type of cover should be noted in the comments section.

2. Assess small and large woody debris along a 1m belt along the transect (1 m upstream and downstream of the transect), dividing the belt into left and right side of center (Figure 2). Small woody debris is defined as being less than or equal to 10 cm in diameter at its largest end, and large woody debris is greater than 10 cm in diameter at its largest end.

3. Fish cover along the banks is assessed within 1 meter upstream and downstream of the transect. Cover along the banks include trees/roots, overhanging vegetation, undercut banks, and bluffs (within 5 m of wetted edge).

**Bank Habitat Data:**

The bank is defined as the area of steep sloping ground bordering the stream that confines the water within the channel at normal water levels, and is located between the channel and the floodplain (Figure 4, Fitzpatrick *et al.*, 1998). The floodplain is defined as a flat or gently sloping depositional area adjacent to the stream. At low flows, it may be difficult to determine the location of the bank due to the presence of bars. Bars are defined as areas usually devoid of woody vegetation (such as small trees and shrubs), and contain coarse materials such as large gravel or cobble. These areas will be covered by water during normal flow and therefore are not considered part of the bank. Each bank measurement begins at the "true" bank (*i.e.*, area of steep slope). In some instances the bank will begin at the wetted edge. If gravel or sand bars are present at a transect, they will not be included in the bank assessment, but will be noted in the comments section by recording the length of the bar from water's edge to the bank.

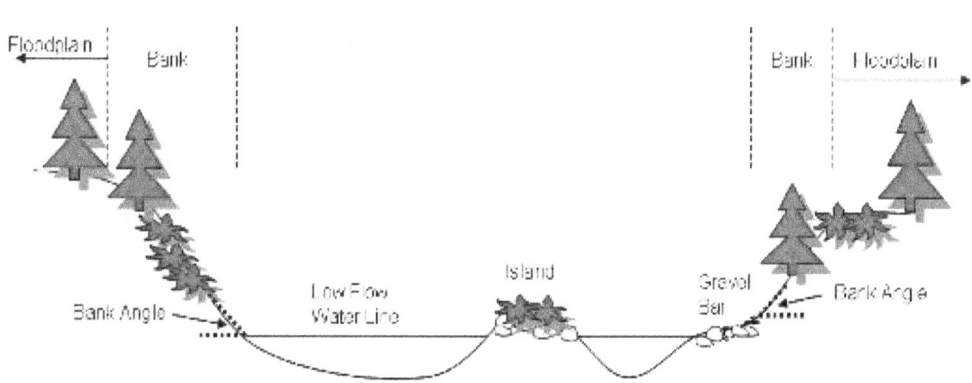

Figure 4. Illustration showing banks and floodplains of a stream.

1. Assess bank stability at each transect and record the category for each characteristic (see Bank Measurement form). Bank characteristics used to measure bank stability are: Angle, Substrate, Percent Vegetative Cover, and Height.

   a. Bank angle and substrate are observed from the bottom of the bank (*i.e.*, at wetted edge or at the top base of the bar, if one is present), and the category code is recorded. To assess the bank substrate, the Wentworth scale is used to visually estimate the dominant substrate type, and the corresponding category code on the data sheet (**not** the Wentworth code) is recorded.
   b. Percent vegetative cover and bank height are assessed from the bank bottom to 10 meters into the bank.

2. Assess bank cover for each bank from the bottom of the bank to 10 meters into the bank. Bank cover categories include large trees, small trees/shrubs, grass/forbs, bare sediment, and artificial cover. If artificial cover is present on the bank (*i.e.*, rip-rap, concrete structures), the type of cover should be noted in the comments section. Note: For bank cover, more than one cover type may be recorded if two cover types are relatively equal in abundance.

## IV. Miscellaneous Actions

1. Record any necessary notes about the collection site or specific samples.

2. Take digital photographs of the reach sampled from upstream and downstream perspectives at mid-channel.

# PHYSICAL HABITAT FORM –SEINED PARKS

Park: _____ Stream # _____ Stream Reach : _____ Date: _____ Time: _____

Measured parameters (Static Core 5 readings taken at TAPR only):

| | Site 1 | Site 2 | Site 3 | Site 4 | Site 5 |
|---|---|---|---|---|---|
| | | | | | |
| Site Type (riffle, run, pool, glide) | | | | | |
| Air temperature (°C) | | | | | |
| Water temperature (°C) | | | | | |
| Secchi visibility (cm) | | | | | |
| Dissolved Oxygen (mg/l) | | | | | |
| Conductivity (uS) | | | | | |
| Relative Conductivity (uS) | | | | | |
| pH | | | | | |

Site dimensions (maximum of 5 sites sampled within a stream reach – 3 widths & depths per site):

| | Site 1 | Site 2 | Site 3 | Site 4 | Site 5 |
|---|---|---|---|---|---|
| Length (m) | | | | | |
| Width 1 (m) | | | | | |
| Width 2 (m) | | | | | |
| Width 3 (m) | | | | | |
| Depth 1 (cm) | | | | | |
| Depth 2 (cm) | | | | | |
| Depth 3 (cm) | | | | | |
| Velocity 1 (m/s) | | | | | |
| Velocity 2 (m/s) | | | | | |
| Velocity 3 (m/s) | | | | | |

Site Substrate (percent category)

| | Site 1 | Site 2 | Site 3 | Site 4 | Site 5 |
|---|---|---|---|---|---|
| Muck | | | | | |
| Detritus | | | | | |
| Silt | | | | | |
| Sand | | | | | |
| Pea-gravel | | | | | |
| Coarse-gravel | | | | | |
| Cobble | | | | | |
| Boulder | | | | | |
| Bedrock | | | | | |
| Hardpan/shale | | | | | |
| Stable (S) | | | | | |
| Unstable (U) | | | | | |
| Comments: | | | | | |

( 0 = none, 1 = trace, 2 = 1 – 5%, 3 = 5 – 25%, 4 = 25 – 50%, 5 = 50 – 75%, 6 = 75 – 95%, 7 = 95 – 100% coverage)

Riparian Cover (dominant cover type)

| | Site 1 | Site 2 | Site 3 | Site 4 | Site 5 |
|---|---|---|---|---|---|
| Right Bank | | | | | |
| 0-25m | | | | | |
| >25-50m | | | | | |
| >50-75m | | | | | |
| >75-100m | | | | | |
| >100m | | | | | |
| Left Bank | | | | | |
| 0-25m | | | | | |
| >25-50m | | | | | |
| >50-75m | | | | | |
| >75-100m | | | | | |
| >100m | | | | | |

COVER TYPES: Mature woodland =1, Woody shrubs/saplings = 2, Wetland/native grasses & forbes (prairie) = 3, Domestic grass, pasture, hay = 4 Park/lawn = 5, Row crop = 6, Road/railroad = 7, Urban/industrial = 8, Other (note in comments) = 9

## Streambank erosion percent

| | Site 1 | Site 2 | Site 3 | Site 4 | Site 5 |
|---|---|---|---|---|---|
| *Right bank* | | | | | |
| Left Bank | | | | | |

GPS (Yes / No): 1__ 2__ 3__ 4__ 5__ stream reach only __

Park: _____          Stream Name: _____          Stream #: _____          Reach: _____

Date: Reac _____          h Length: _____          Transect Spacing (reach length / 10): _____          Crew: _____

| Trans | Channel Unit | Pool Form | Width (m) | Depth (cm) | Velocity (m/sec) | Dominant ** Substrate | Embededness | Canopy Cover |
|---|---|---|---|---|---|---|---|---|
| 1* | | | | Lt<br>Ctr<br>Rt | Lt<br>Ctr<br>Rt | Lt<br>Ctr<br>Rt | Lt<br>Ctr<br>Rt | Lt<br>Ctr<br>Rt |
| 2 | | | | Lt<br>Ctr<br>Rt | Lt<br>Ctr<br>Rt | Lt<br>Ctr<br>Rt | Lt<br>Ctr<br>Rt | Lt<br>Ctr<br>Rt |
| 3 | | | | Lt<br>Ctr<br>Rt | Lt<br>Ctr<br>Rt | Lt<br>Ctr<br>Rt | Lt<br>Ctr<br>Rt | Lt<br>Ctr<br>Rt |
| 4 | | | | Lt<br>Ctr<br>Rt | Lt<br>Ctr<br>Rt | Lt<br>Ctr<br>Rt | Lt<br>Ctr<br>Rt | Lt<br>Ctr<br>Rt |
| 5 | | | | Lt<br>Ctr<br>Rt | Lt<br>Ctr<br>Rt | Lt<br>Ctr<br>Rt | Lt<br>Ctr<br>Rt | Lt<br>Ctr<br>Rt |
| 6 | | | | Lt<br>Ctr<br>Rt | Lt<br>Ctr<br>Rt | Lt<br>Ctr<br>Rt | Lt<br>Ctr<br>Rt | Lt<br>Ctr<br>Rt |
| 7 | | | | Lt<br>Ctr<br>Rt | Lt<br>Ctr<br>Rt | Lt<br>Ctr<br>Rt | Lt<br>Ctr<br>Rt | Lt<br>Ctr<br>Rt |
| 8 | | | | Lt<br>Ctr<br>Rt | Lt<br>Ctr<br>Rt | Lt<br>Ctr<br>Rt | Lt<br>Ctr<br>Rt | Lt<br>Ctr<br>Rt |
| 9 | | | | Lt<br>Ctr<br>Rt | Lt<br>Ctr<br>Rt | Lt<br>Ctr<br>Rt | Lt<br>Ctr<br>Rt | Lt<br>Ctr<br>Rt |
| 10 | | | | Lt<br>Ctr<br>Rt | Lt<br>Ctr<br>Rt | Lt<br>Ctr<br>Rt | Lt<br>Ctr<br>Rt | Lt<br>Ctr<br>Rt |
| 11 | | | | Lt<br>Ctr<br>Rt | Lt<br>Ctr<br>Rt | Lt<br>Ctr<br>Rt | Lt<br>Ctr<br>Rt | Lt<br>Ctr<br>Rt |

| CHANNEL UNIT CODES | | POOL FORM CODES | | Embededness & Canopy Cover |
|---|---|---|---|---|
| GL | Glide | B | Backwater Pool | 0 = Absent (0%) |
| RI | Riffle | F | Bluff Pool | 1 = Sparse (<10%) |
| RU | Run/Race | I | Impoundment | 2 = Moderate (10-40%) |
| PO | Pool | L | Lateral Pool | 3 = Heavy (40-75%) |
| RRX | Riffle-Run complex | M | Mid-Channel Pool | 4 = Very Heavy (>75%) |
| PGX | Pool-Glide complex | O | Obstruction Pool | (Canopy within 1m on each side of transect) |

*Transects are equally spaced as determined by dividing the reach length by 10.

   Transect 1 is located at the downstream end of the reach; Transect 11 is located at the upstream end of the reach

** Dominate substrate is average substrate within a 10 cm diameter circle around the point where depth is taken

Embeddness is assessed within a 10 cm diameter circle around point

**Fish Cover Form -Electrofished Reaches**

Page ____ of ____

Park:      Stream Name:      Stream #:      Reach:

Date:      Reach Length:      Transect Spacing Interval:      Crew:

| Trans. | | Fish Cover* Circle all cover types present. | | | | | | | | | | Comment |
|---|---|---|---|---|---|---|---|---|---|---|---|---|
| 1 | Lt | FA | HY | BO | AR | SWD | LWD | T/R | OV | UC | BL | |
| | Ctr | FA | HY | BO | AR | | | | | | | |
| | Rt | FA | HY | BO | AR | SWD | LWD | T/R | OV | UC | BL | |
| 2 | Lt | FA | HY | BO | AR | SWD | LWD | T/R | OV | UC | BL | |
| | Ctr | FA | HY | BO | AR | | | | | | | |
| | Rt | FA | HY | BO | AR | SWD | LWD | T/R | OV | UC | BL | |
| 3 | Lt | FA | HY | BO | AR | SWD | LWD | T/R | OV | UC | BL | |
| | Ctr | FA | HY | BO | AR | | | | | | | |
| | Rt | FA | HY | BO | AR | SWD | LWD | T/R | OV | UC | BL | |
| 4 | Lt | FA | HY | BO | AR | SWD | LWD | T/R | OV | UC | BL | |
| | Ctr | FA | HY | BO | AR | | | | | | | |
| | Rt | FA | HY | BO | AR | SWD | LWD | T/R | OV | UC | BL | |
| 5 | Lt | FA | HY | BO | AR | SWD | LWD | T/R | OV | UC | BL | |
| | Ctr | FA | HY | BO | AR | | | | | | | |
| | Rt | FA | HY | BO | AR | SWD | LWD | T/R | OV | UC | BL | |
| 6 | Lt | FA | HY | BO | AR | SWD | LWD | T/R | OV | UC | BL | |
| | Ctr | FA | HY | BO | AR | | | | | | | |
| | Rt | FA | HY | BO | AR | SWD | LWD | T/R | OV | UC | BL | |
| 7 | Lt | FA | HY | BO | AR | SWD | LWD | T/R | OV | UC | BL | |
| | Ctr | FA | HY | BO | AR | | | | | | | |
| | Rt | FA | HY | BO | AR | SWD | LWD | T/R | OV | UC | BL | |
| 8 | Lt | FA | HY | BO | AR | SWD | LWD | T/R | OV | UC | BL | |
| | Ctr | FA | HY | BO | AR | | | | | | | |
| | Rt | FA | HY | BO | AR | SWD | LWD | T/R | OV | UC | BL | |
| 9 | Lt | FA | HY | BO | AR | SWD | LWD | T/R | OV | UC | BL | |
| | Ctr | FA | HY | BO | AR | | | | | | | |
| | Rt | FA | HY | BO | AR | SWD | LWD | T/R | OV | UC | BL | |
| 10 | Lt | FA | HY | BO | AR | SWD | LWD | T/R | OV | UC | BL | |
| | Ctr | FA | HY | BO | AR | | | | | | | |
| | Rt | FA | HY | BO | AR | SWD | LWD | T/R | OV | UC | BL | |
| 11 | Lt | FA | HY | BO | AR | SWD | LWD | T/R | OV | UC | BL | |
| | Ctr | FA | HY | BO | AR | | | | | | | |
| | Rt | FA | HY | BO | AR | SWD | LWD | T/R | OV | UC | BL | |

| Fish Cover Types* | Additional comments: |
|---|---|
| FA = Filamentous Algae | |
| HY = Hydrophytes & Mosses | |
| BO = Boulders | |
| AR = Artificial | |
| | **FA, HY, BO, AR are assessed within a 10cm diameter circle around each point on transect** |
| SWD = Small Woody Debris | **SWD is < 10 cm in diameter at largest end; LWD is >10 cm at largest end** |
| LWD = Large Woody Debris | **SWD & LWD assessed on a 1m belt along transect on left and right side of center of channel** |
| T/R = Trees/Roots | **T/R, OV, UC, BL are assessed within 1 m on either side of transect along bank** |
| OV = Overhanging Veg | |
| UC = Undercut bank | |
| BL = Bluff within 5m of water | |

**10 cm or 0.1m**

70

# Bank Measurment Form - Electrofished Reaches

Park: S      tream Name:      Stream #:      Reach:

Date:      Reach Length:      Transect Spacing Interval:      Crew:

| Trans. | | Bank Stability | | | | Bank Cover* Circle Dominant (>50%) Cover | | | | | Comment |
|--------|----|-------|-----|--------|-----|----|----|----|----|----|---------|
| | | Angle | Veg | Height | Sub | | | | | | |
| 1 | Lt | | | | | TR | SH | GR | BA | AR | |
| | Rt | | | | | TR | SH | GR | BA | AR | |
| 2 | Lt | | | | | TR | SH | GR | BA | AR | |
| | Rt | | | | | TR | SH | GR | BA | AR | |
| 3 | Lt | | | | | TR | SH | GR | BA | AR | |
| | Rt | | | | | TR | SH | GR | BA | AR | |
| 4 | Lt | | | | | TR | SH | GR | BA | AR | |
| | Rt | | | | | TR | SH | GR | BA | AR | |
| 5 | Lt | | | | | TR | SH | GR | BA | AR | |
| | Rt | | | | | TR | SH | GR | BA | AR | |
| 6 | Lt | | | | | TR | SH | GR | BA | AR | |
| | Rt | | | | | TR | SH | GR | BA | AR | |
| 7 | Lt | | | | | TR | SH | GR | BA | AR | |
| | Rt | | | | | TR | SH | GR | BA | AR | |
| 8 | Lt | | | | | TR | SH | GR | BA | AR | |
| | Rt | | | | | TR | SH | GR | BA | AR | |
| 9 | Lt | | | | | TR | SH | GR | BA | AR | |
| | Rt | | | | | TR | SH | GR | BA | AR | |
| 10 | Lt | | | | | TR | SH | GR | BA | AR | |
| | Rt | | | | | TR | SH | GR | BA | AR | |
| 11 | Lt | | | | | TR | SH | GR | BA | AR | |
| | Rt | | | | | TR | SH | GR | BA | AR | |

*Bank cover is assessed within 1 m on each side of transect and 10 m up the bank from wetted edge

| Bank Angle, Degrees | Vegetative Cover (%) | Height (m) | Substrate | Bank Cover Types* |
|--------|--------|--------|--------|--------|
| 1 = 0 - 30 | 1 = >80 | 1 = 0-1 | 1 = Bedrock/Artificial | TR = Large trees (> 3 in. dbh) |
| 2 = 31-60 | 2 = 50-80 | 2 = 1.1-2 | 2 = Boulder/Cobble | SH = Small trees and shrubs |
| 3 = >60 | 3 = 20-49 | 3 = 2.1-3 | 5 = Silt | GR = Grass and Forbes |
| | 4 = <20 | 4 = 3.1-4 | 8 = Sand | BA = Bare rock/sediment |
| | | 5 = >4 | 10 = Gravel/Sand | AR = Artificial |

## Bank Angles

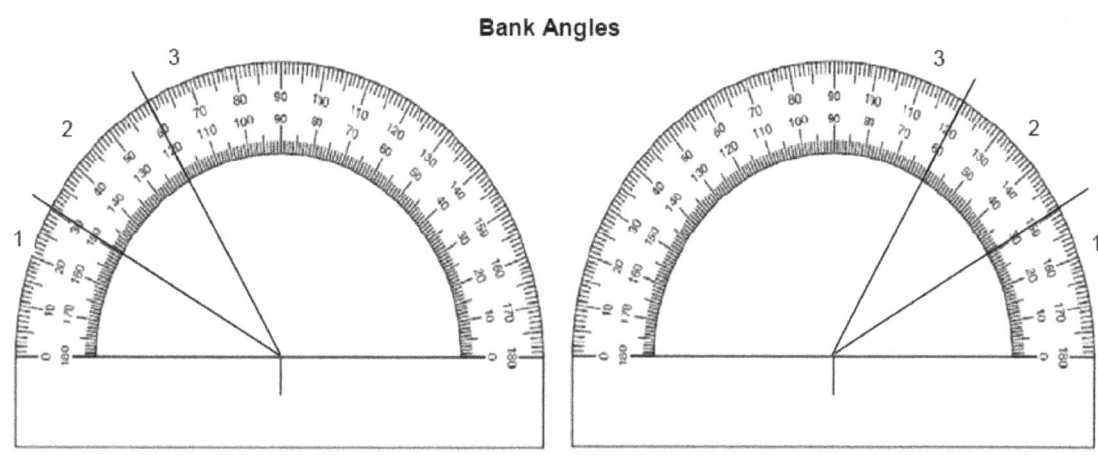

71

# WENTWORTH SUBSTRATE CODES

1= <0.062 (silt/clay)
2= 0.062-0.125 (very fine sand
3= 0.125-0.25 (fine sand)

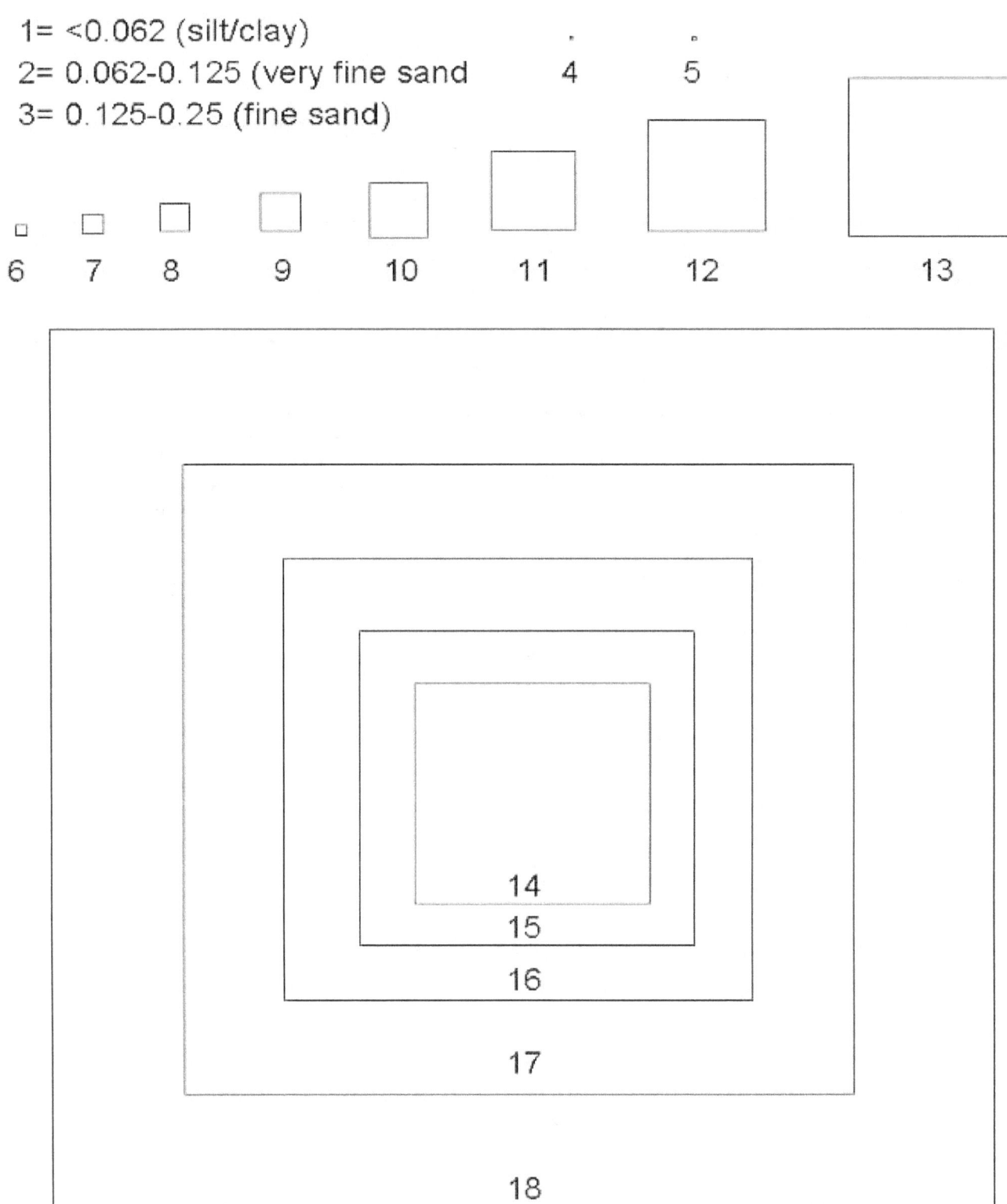

4    5

6    7    8    9    10    11    12    13

14
15
16
17
18

**19**=180-256 mm, **20**=256-362 mm, **21**=362-512 mm, **22**=512-1024 mm, **23**= >1024 mm, **24**=Bedrock

# Protocol for Monitoring Fish Communities in Small Streams in the Heartland Inventory and Monitoring Network

## SOP 6:  Measuring Stream Discharge

## Version 1.00 (05/01/2008)

**Revision History Log:**

| Previous Version # | Revision Date | Author | Changes Made | Reason for Change | New Version # |
|---|---|---|---|---|---|
|  |  |  |  |  |  |
|  |  |  |  |  |  |
|  |  |  |  |  |  |
|  |  |  |  |  |  |
|  |  |  |  |  |  |

This SOP is guidance for measuring discharge in wadeable streams. The SOP describes sampling procedures, calibration, and general maintenance procedures. If other meters are used, field personnel should review the instruction manual for instrument-specific guidance on how to calibrate and operate those particular meters.

## I. Background Information

Velocity and depth are measured using a current meter attached to a wading rod. The rod allows for quick and easy measurements of depth with incremental markings, and has an adjustable arm that places the current meter at the proper depth for measuring velocity (60% of the depth from the surface of the water; Carter and Davidian, 1969). Some current meters have rotating cups (Pygmy and Price models) while others have a pair of electronic contacts on a small head (FLO-MATE 2000) to measure velocity. The sensor in the Marsh-McBirney FLO-MATE 2000 is equipped with an electromagnetic coil that produces a magnetic field. A pair of carbon electrodes measure the voltage produced by the velocity of the conductor, which in this case is the flowing water. Internal electronics process measured voltages and output them as linear measurements of velocity. Velocity is displayed as either feet per second or meters per second.

Stream discharge (Q) is the volume of water passing a cross-section per unit of time and is generally expressed in cubic feet per second ($ft^3/s$) or cubic meters per second ($m^3/sec$). Discharge is estimated by multiplying current velocity by the cross-sectional area (Carter and Davidian, 1969). Cross sectional area is determined by first measuring the width of the stream channel. The cross section is then divided into smaller increments (usually 15 to 20 intervals) and depth and velocity are measured at each increment. The depth and width of the interval are multiplied to get an area for each interval and then each interval area and velocity is multiplied to produce a discharge for each interval. These discharges are summed to produce a total discharge for that cross section of the stream. This process will be described in greater, step-by-step detail in the "Procedures" section.

## II. Prior to the Field

1. Standard wading rods come in both metric and English standard units (feet). Whatever units are used, ensure that there is consistency between the settings on the velocity meter, the wading rod, and the tape measure, and that the units are clearly recorded on the data sheet. English standard units are easily converted to metric units when required.

2. Ensure new batteries are placed in units that require them.

3. Calibrate velocity meters (FLO-MATE 2000 or USGS pygmy) according to instructions in the manufacturer's operations manuals. Photocopies of the operations manuals should be taken to the field.

4. Equipment maintenance and storage should follow guidance issued by the manufacturers.

## III. In the Field

Discharge measurements require wading across the stream and may stir up sediments, disrupting accurate measurement of other parameters.

Quantitative Discharge Procedure:

1. Prior to taking any measurements, the location where discharge will be measured must be determined. An ideal cross-section in the sample reach will have the following qualities:

   a. The stream channel directly above and below the cross-section is straight.

   b. There is measurable stream flow, with a stream depth preferably greater than 10 cm and velocities generally greater than 0.15 meter/second.

   c. The streambed is a uniform "U" shape, free of large boulders, woody debris, and dense aquatic vegetation.

   d. The stream flow is laminar and relatively uniform with no eddies, backwaters, or excessive turbulence.
      Note: The cross section will not likely meet all these qualifications but the best location should be selected based on these standards. Record (or draw a diagram) on the data sheet a description of any discrepancies with the cross section.

2. Once the cross section is established, measure the width of the stream with a tape measure to the nearest 0.1 meter and secure the tape across the stream for the duration of the discharge measurement.

3. Divide the stream into equal intervals across the width of the cross section, usually 15 to 20. A minimum of 10 intervals is recommended. A velocity and depth measurement will be recorded for each interval across the stream at the center of each interval. For example, if the

stream is 10 meters wide, 10 velocity and depth measurements will be taken at one meter intervals. The first measurement will be taken a half meter from the water's edge, the second will be taken at 1 ½ m from the water's edge, etc., as shown in Figure 1.

4.  Attach the sensor to the wading rod and ensure that the sensor is securely screwed onto the rod and facing upright.

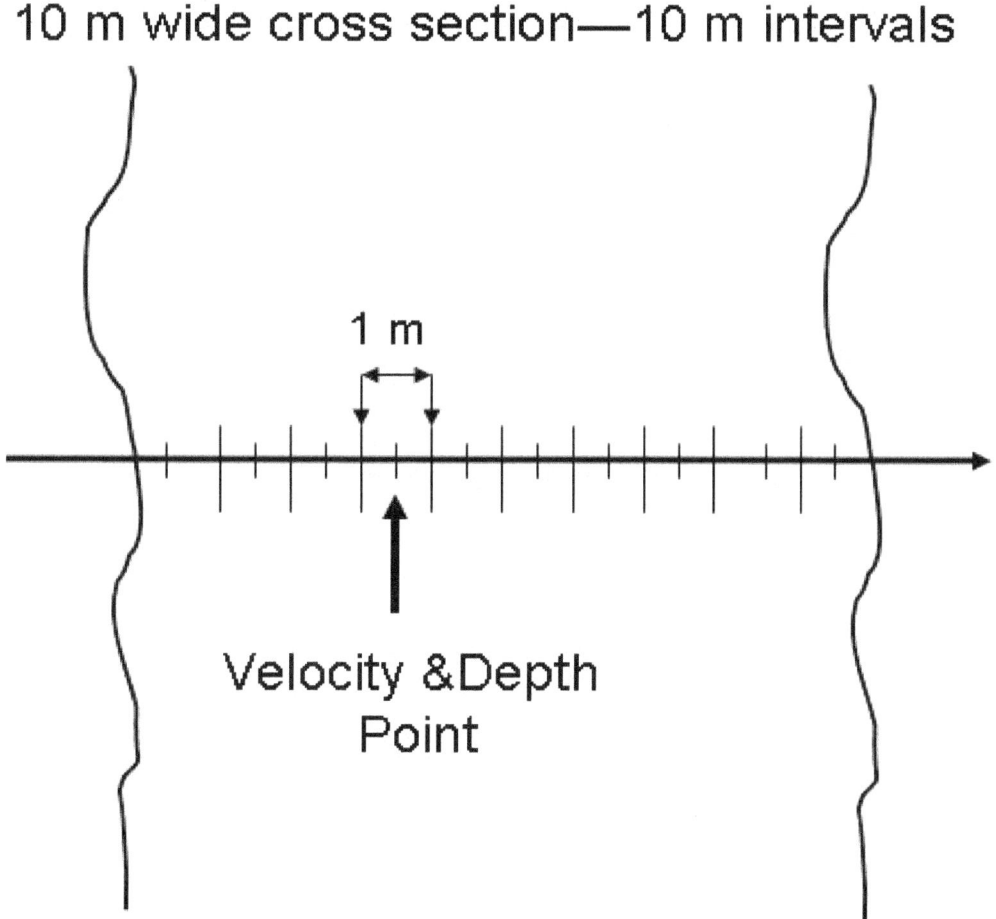

Figure 1. Cross section diagram.

5.  One person should measure discharge and one person should remain on the bank, recording data. The first readings are taken at water's edge and are recorded as depth=0 and velocity =0. Proceed to the next interval and record readings. Place the wading rod as level as possible and hold perpendicular to the water level. Read depth from the wading rod to the nearest centimeter. The rod will have graduated marks along its length, with single marks indicating two centimeters, double marks indicating 10 centimeters, and triple marks indicating one-half meter increments.

6. Once depth has been read, adjust the arm of the sliding rod with the sensor attached to 60% of the water depth. The wading rod will place the sensor at 60% of the depth from the surface of the water when properly adjusted. <u>Note</u>: For example, if the depth is 2.6 meters, line up the 2 on the meter scale (sliding rod) with the 6 on the tenth scale (increments on handle of fixed rod). The sensor is now located at 60% of the water depth.

7. Stand behind the sensor and make sure there is no disturbance (including the senor cord) around the sensor that interferes with the velocity measurement. The meter may be adjusted slightly up or downstream to avoid boulders or other interferences. <u>Note</u>: Make sure the sensor directly faces the flow of the water. This may not always be directly parallel with the water's edge; the rod and sensor may need to be turned slightly with each measurement.

8. Allow the instrument enough time to get an accurate reading--generally around a minute. Watch the time bar complete two full cycles and then take the velocity reading. If something happens during the measurement, such as accidental movement of the wading rod, the reading should be repeated.

9. Call out the distance from the water's edge, the depth, and then the velocity to the person recording data. Continue moving across the stream until measurements have been taken at all intervals. <u>Note:</u> If the water velocity increases greatly between intervals, additional measurements can be taken to shorten the width of the intervals within this area of high velocity. Be sure to change the interval width for these measurements in the calculation of discharge.

10. When finished, detach the sensor from the wading rod and place it back in the storage bag or case for transportation. If you do not expect to use the meter for several days, turn the meter off, clean the sensor, and store properly.

# Discharge

Park: _____     Stream name:_____

Stream #:_____          Reach:_____

Date:_____ Time:_____ Crew Initials:_____

Stream width:_____ft or m     Meter used:_____

| Interval | Interval Width ft or m | Depth Vel ft or cm | ocity ft/s or m/s |
|---|---|---|---|
| 1 | | | |
| 2 | | | |
| 3 | | | |
| 4 | | | |
| 5 | | | |
| 6 | | | |
| 7 | | | |
| 8 | | | |
| 9 | | | |
| 10 | | | |
| 11 | | | |
| 12 | | | |
| 13 | | | |
| 14 | | | |
| 15 | | | |
| 16 | | | |
| 17 | | | |
| 18 | | | |
| 19 | | | |
| 20 | | | |

## Notes:

## SOP 7: Equipment Storage and Maintenance after the Field Season

### Version 1.00 (05/01/2008)

**Revision History Log:**

| Previous Version # | Revision Date | Author | Changes Made | Reason for Change | New Version # |
|---|---|---|---|---|---|
|  |  |  |  |  |  |
|  |  |  |  |  |  |
|  |  |  |  |  |  |
|  |  |  |  |  |  |
|  |  |  |  |  |  |

Maintenance of sampling equipment will be necessary to maximize its life and ensure proper functioning. Poorly maintained equipment adversely affects equipment performance, decreasing the accuracy of water quality readings and sampling efficiency. This will introduce variability into the data set. This SOP explains procedures that all field observers should be familiar with and follow after the field season is completed.

## I. Procedures:

### Equipment

1. Clean and repair all equipment prior to return to the proper storage areas. Maintenance and storage of electronic equipment should follow manufacturer's instructions.

2. Check sampling nets and determine if new nets must be ordered prior to the next field season.

3. Batteries must be removed from all equipment. Rechargeable batteries are used in some equipment (*e.g.*, backpack electrofishing units). These batteries should remain on chargers when not in use.

4. Clean the inside and outside of all vehicles used in the field.

### Paperwork and Reports

1. All reference manuals should be re-shelved. Other reference materials and extra data sheets need to be filed in their appropriate filing cabinet.

2. At the end of each field season, after all sampling has been completed, the project manager will file a trip report with the data manager outlining hours worked, field-crew members and their responsibilities on the project, and any unique situations encountered. This information is incorporated in the database and used during data analysis, and it may be useful in identifying causes for discrepancies and inconsistencies in the data.

## SOP 8: Data Management

## Version 1.00 (05/01/2008)

**Revision History Log:**

| Previous Version # | Revision Date | Author | Changes Made | Reason for Change | New Version # |
|---|---|---|---|---|---|
|  |  |  |  |  |  |
|  |  |  |  |  |  |
|  |  |  |  |  |  |
|  |  |  |  |  |  |
|  |  |  |  |  |  |

This SOP describes procedures for managing the Heartland Network (HTLN) monitoring database for small stream fish communities. The database is called 'Stfish'. Specifically, this document addresses procedures for data entry, verification, validation, export to outside systems, security and availability. Parks are referenced throughout the database using the standard National Park Service four-letter abbreviations. Database users should become familiar with the park abbreviations. Park names, abbreviations and links to internet URLs are available through the opening form (the "Switchboard") of the database.

Database design is critical to understanding how to use a database effectively. This SOP describes database design issues that have been addressed by the NPS Inventory and Monitoring (I&M) Program (NPS, 2006) and database design issues specific to the small stream fish database. Data management can be divided into: (a) the initial design phase that involves defining the data model, its entities and their relationships, and (b) the procedures necessary to implement the database. Microsoft (MS) Access 2003 is the primary software used for maintaining fish community data. Water quality data will be stored in the National Park Service's NPStoret database (NPS-WRD, 2007). Environmental Systems Research Institute (ESRI) ArcInfo 9.x is used for managing spatial data associated with field sampling locations. Data products derived from this project will be available at the NPS I&M Data Store and EPA Storet National Data Warehouse. QA/QC guidelines in this document are based on recommendations of Rowell *et al*. (2005) and citations therein.

## I. Data Model

Stfish has a hierarchical design based on Natural Resource Database Template (NRDT). Locations (reaches) and sampling periods are maintained at the top (they relate one-to-many with other tables in the database). Stfish is the product of two databases linked together by location and sampling season. The databases represent two field sampling methods: seining and electrofishing.

Currently, sampling at PIPE, TAPR, and HOME is limited to seining while electrofishing is used at EFMO, GWCA, HEHO, HOSP, PERI, and WICR.

The Stfish database contains 36 primary data tables (excluding look-up, enumeration and reference tables). To simplify data management, Stfish is designed with a table-naming system containing two prefixes: tables for seining data have the prefix "tbl_" while tables containing data from electrofishing samples have the prefix "etbl_".

Sampling periods (tbl_SamplingPeriods), locations (tbl_Locations), seining events (tbl_SamplingEvents) and electrofish events (etbl_Reach) form the core tables. The core tables capture the field sample occasion (the when and where of the sample). Field data tables link to these core tables. An entity relationship diagram of the basic design is given in Figure 1. The figure depicts information such as date and time, reach name, and park/project codes. It also includes detailed fish monitoring information pertaining to the community sampled in tbl_FishObservations and etbl_FishCommSppIndiv. Other tables include habitat data (*e.g.*, substrate, discharge, stream dimensions), and associated lookup tables (*e.g.*, Wentworth substrate codes, taxonomic data). The diagram shows the basic similarities and differences between the seining portion and the electrofishing portions of the system (Figure 1).

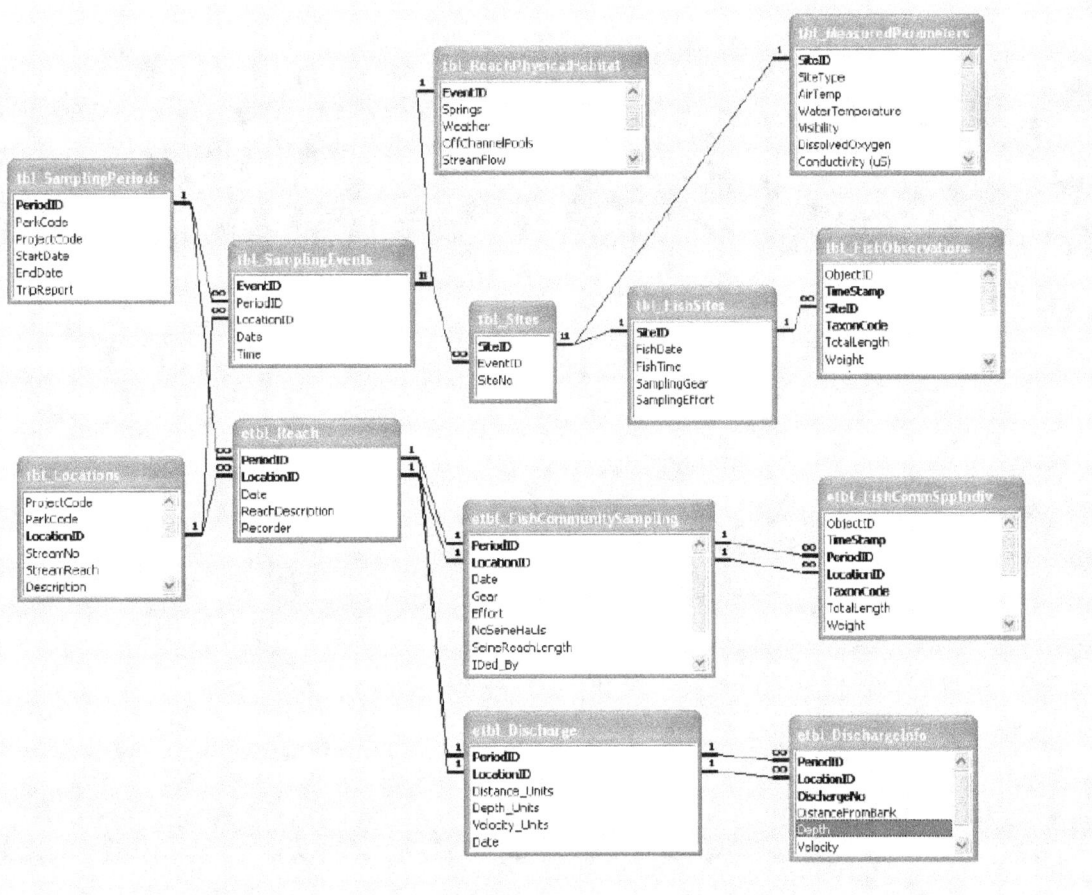

Figure 1. Data model for Stfish. Tables with the prefix "tbl_" indicate seining data (above) while tables with the prefix "etbl_" are electro-fishing data. (below).

## II. Data Preparation

Quality assurance and quality control procedures related to data recording are important components of any project. Sampling data (*i.e.*, sample methods, effort, weather/water quality conditions, and species abundance data) are recorded and checked for completeness either before leaving a site or within 24 hours of data recording. This will aid in verification and validation of the data after entry into the database. To prevent the complete loss of field form data due to unforeseen circumstances (*i.e.*, fire or flood in the workplace), all field sheets are photocopied and a hard copy located in a separate location as the original. Field sheets are scanned into a computer and electronic copies of the data sheets stored on the HTLN server located at Missouri State University, Springfield, MO. This will ensure that at least one copy of the field sheets is available for data entry and verification.

## III. Data Entry

Data entry is accomplished using Access forms and tables. Upon opening the database, the switchboard appears (Figure 2). Navigate to each data-entry form using the switchboard. An overview of the major data-entry forms is given in Figure 3.

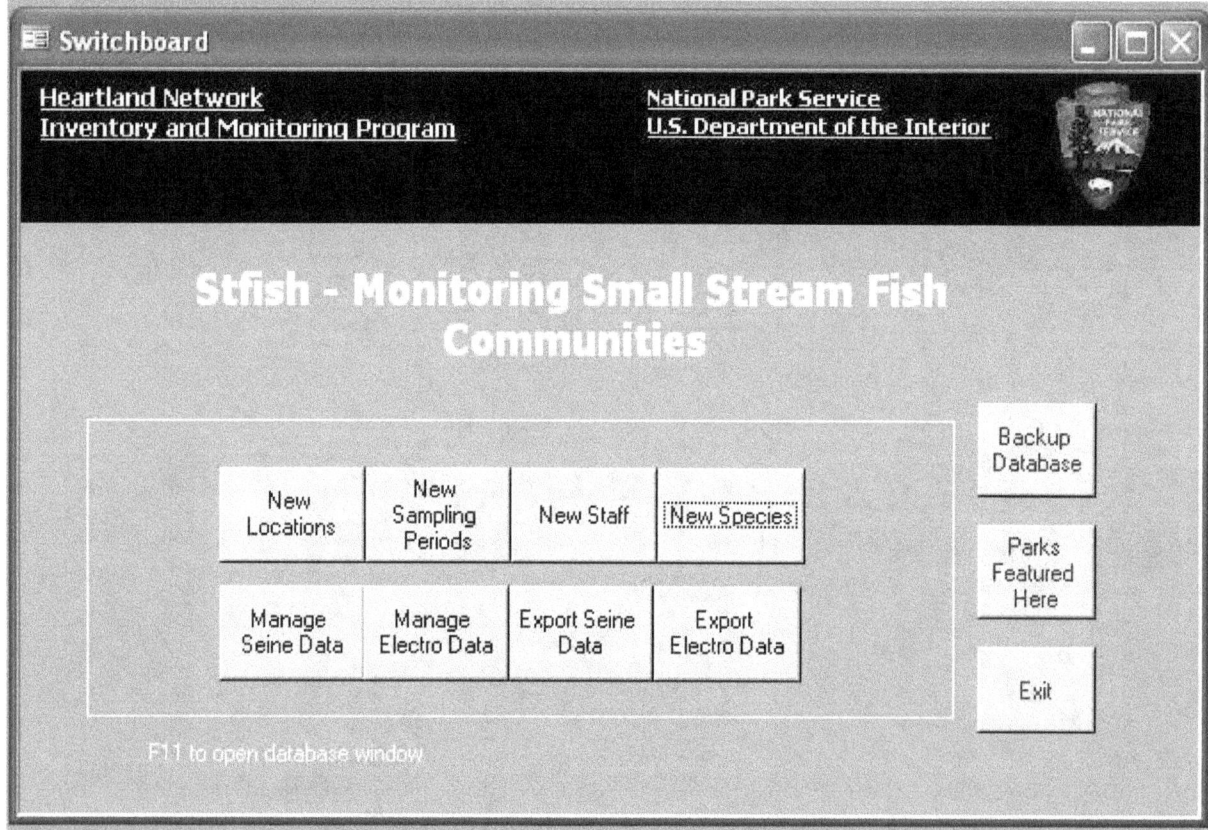

Figure 2. Stfish database switchboard.

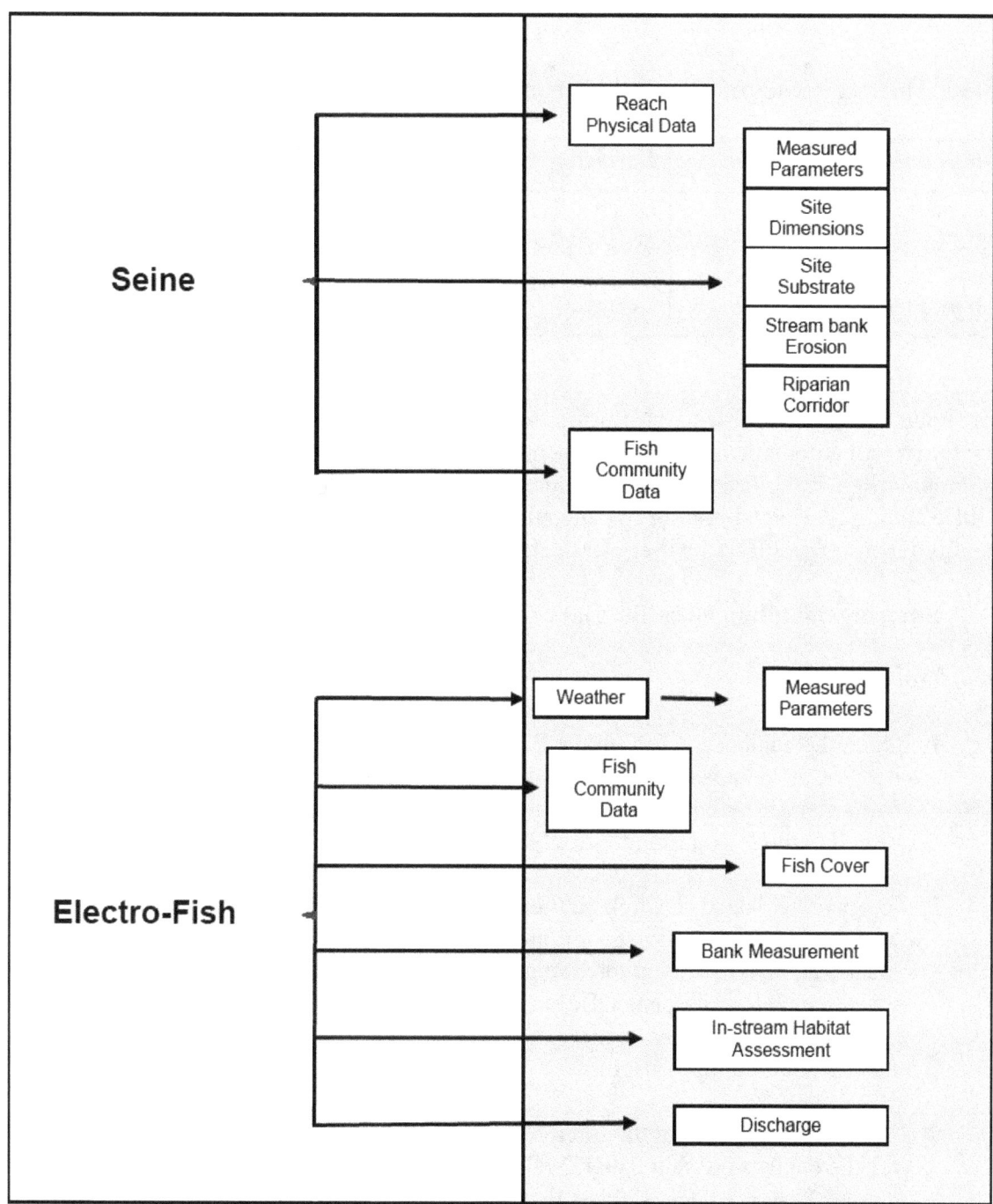

Figure 3. Outline of stream fish data forms. Note: Forms are selected from the main switchboard (seine or electro-fish buttons) and data are entered into subforms (shaded area).

## Seine Data Entry

Seine data entry is a derived process from the legacy Shiner database (Peitz and Rowell, 2004). EventID and SiteID fields are derived from LocationID and PeriodID. Locality and time information for monitoring data are stored in *key fields* of the location and sampling period and sampling event tables (see Table 1). A key is a column in a table dedicated to linking to other tables. In other words, keys are the fields that create the relationships between tables.

Table 1. Three key fields used in the Stfish database are shown.

| Table Name | Key Field | Example (record value) |
|---|---|---|
| tbl_Location | LocationID | PIPEShiner01above |
| tbl_SamplingPeriod | PeriodID | PIPEShiner2006Aug29 |
| tbl_SamplingEvent | EventID | PIPEShiner2006Aug300750 |

Staff should add new records to tbl_Location only when new sampling sites are established. Data-entry forms will automatically generate EventID values. The main area of concern is the tbl_SamplingPeriod table. Staff should ensure that the necessary PeriodID record is included in the tbl_SamplingPeriod table prior to data entry. After inputting sampling occasion data (LocationID and PeriodID), the user can begin to enter additional fish community data.

**Entering Sampling Occasion Data**

Procedures:

1. Open the database. Click on the Backup Database button to the left. This will save a copy of the database including today's date in the filename. Store your backups in some standard location that will be copied to tape or other standard backups periodically. If you run into trouble, you can fall back on this copy.

2. Reopen the database. Click on the New Locations button. Verify that all of the locations that you will need for data entry are included on this table. If you have new locations, insert them on the bottom of the table. They will be sorted alphabetically when the table is reopened. Be sure to identify whether the location falls under the project code of 'Shiner' (seining) or 'Stfish' (electro-fish). Close the table by clicking the red X on the upper right.

3. Click on the New Sampling Periods. Verify that there is an entry for the year and park for the data you wish to enter. Make a new entry if required. Close the table by clicking the red X on the upper right of the table.

4. Click on the "Manage Seine Data" button. This will open the main window for entering seine data (see Figure 4).

5. Choose the sampling location and sampling period from those available in the combo box.

   Note: If the sampling location or sampling period value you need is not displayed, return to the switchboard then choose new locations or new sampling periods and update the table(s).

6. Enter the field date and time. EventID will be generated when you tab from the "Time" entry field.

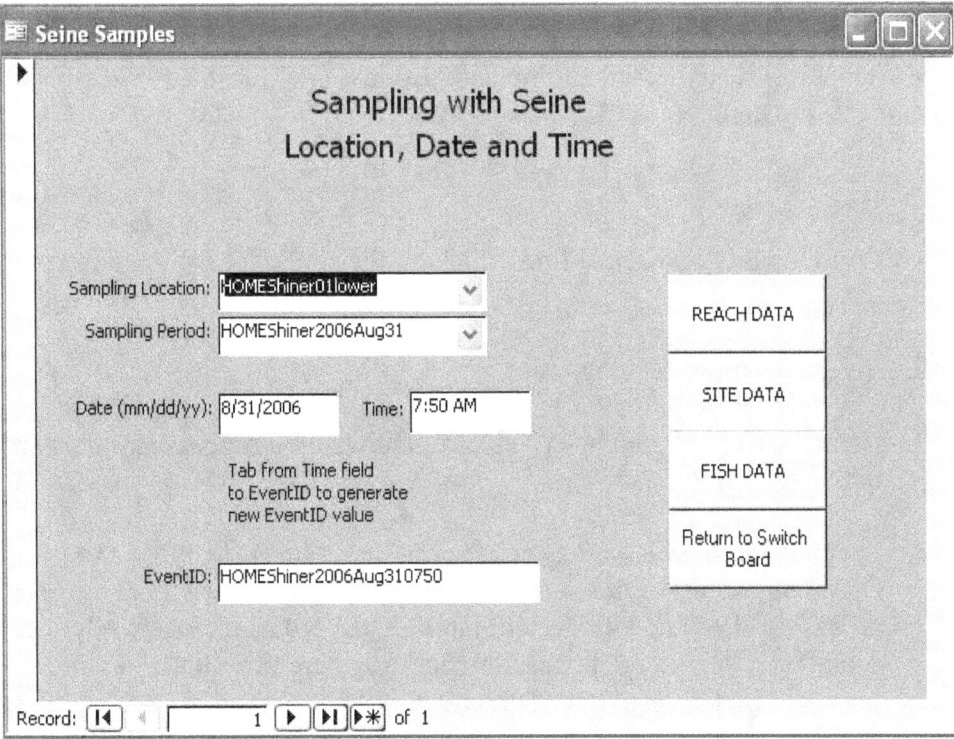

Figure 4. Main window for entering seine data.

**Entering Reach Conditions Data**

Procedures:

1. Click on the Reach Data button (shown in Figure 4).

2. Note that when you click on any of the data entry buttons, the database will acknowledge that you are either creating a new event, returning to a previous session, or creating some error condition owing to a typo in your event information. Proceed with reach data entry.

3. In the reach data form, click on Collectors and enter the staff participating in gathering physical habitat data for the sampled reach.

4. Click on Reach Data to enter reach specific parameters and weather conditions.

5. Return to the main window for entering seine data (shown in Figure 4).

85

**Entering Site Habitat Data**

Site-level data describe the physical habitat for prairie fish communities for up to five sites per reach. SiteIDs are the key fields that maintain site table relationships. SiteID values are automatically generated the first time data are entered. There are seven sections of site-level data: Measured Parameters, Site Dimensions, Site Substrate, Site Substrate Stability, Streambank Erosion Percent, Riparian Corridor, and GPS data.

Procedures:

1. From the Site-level Data form, click on the site-level section that you wish to enter data.

2. Select the appropriate SiteID.

3. Enter each of the parameter values as shown on the field data sheet and the database form for each site.

4. For the Measured Parameters form, enter the SiteID and Site Type for all seined sites. Only CORE 5 measurements from the hand-held meters are entered for sites at TAPR. PIPE and HOME will have CORE 5 data electronically recorded on data sondes (see Water Quality section below); therefore, CORE 5 parameters on this form will be left blank for PIPE and HOME.

5. To move to the next site, hit the Continue button and select the next SiteID from the drop down box. For the Site Substrate Stability and GPS forms, data for multiple sites at a reach can be entered at one time; and therefore, there is no Continue button needed on these forms.

6. To return to the Site-Level Data form, click the Return button.

**Entering Fish Community Data**

Species data are comprised of three types: individually weighed fish, batch weighed fish, and counted fish data. Individual fish consist of 30 individuals of each species that are individually measured (total length) and weighed. Batch weighed fish are smaller species that are individually measured but are weighed in groups. Counted fish are those individuals that are identified and only counted.

Procedures:

1. Starting from the main window for seine data (as shown in Figure 4), click on Fish Data button.

2. Enter the parameters in the text boxes related to sampling, starting with SiteID.

3. Click on Collectors and enter the initials of each staff member. Return to the Individual Fish Data form.

4. Click the Fish Data button and enter the species name for subsequent data entry. Click on Add Individual Data button to enter length and weight data.

5. Individually weighed fish. Enter the total length, weight and anomaly. If no anomalies exist, then enter "N". Indicate if the individual was kept as a voucher (Yes/No) and enter the number of individuals (which will be 1, the default) and any comments for that fish. If the fish is a Topeka shiner, enter the age (J = juvenile, M = mature).

6. Batch weighed fish. Enter the individual length. Omit the weight, enter a batch number, and any anomalies for that individual. If all 30 fish are weighed together, then batch will be "1" for all fish of that species. If multiple batches are weighed for a species, then the first group is batch "1", the second group is batch "2", *etc*. The record for the last fish in the batch will have the batch weight entered under BatchTotalWt. Indicate if the individual was kept as a voucher (Yes/No) and enter the number of individuals (which will be 1, the default) and any comments for that fish.

7. Counted fish. Leave the Length, Weight, Batch, BatchTotalWt, and Age fields blank. Enter only the number of fish counted, any anomalies for the group of fish and indicate if the counted fish were vouchered.

## Electrofish Data Entry

Electro-fish data entry is based on the methods described in Petersen et al., (2008). Table relationships are implemented by way of compound keys. An example of a table with a compound key is 'etbl_DischargeInfo' where the key consists of PeriodID, LocationID, and DischargeNo (see Figure 1). While this makes the design of the database somewhat more complicated, it greatly increases the control over tables and their associated forms during the data entry process.

### Entering Sampling Occasion Data

Procedures:

1. Open the database. Click on the Backup Database button to the right. This will save a copy of the database including today's date in the filename. Store the backups in some standard location that will be copied to tape or other standard backups periodically.

2. Reopen the database. Click on the Manage Electro Data button. This will open the main window for entering electro-fish data (see Figure 5). Data entry for the electro-fish portion of Stfish is managed using unique combinations of LocationID and PeriodID. The desired combination is selected in the main window for electro-fish data entry (Figure 5).

3. Enter date, reach length, reach description, and additional comments if necessary.

4. Click on Recorders button and enter initials. Return to main electro-fishing menu.

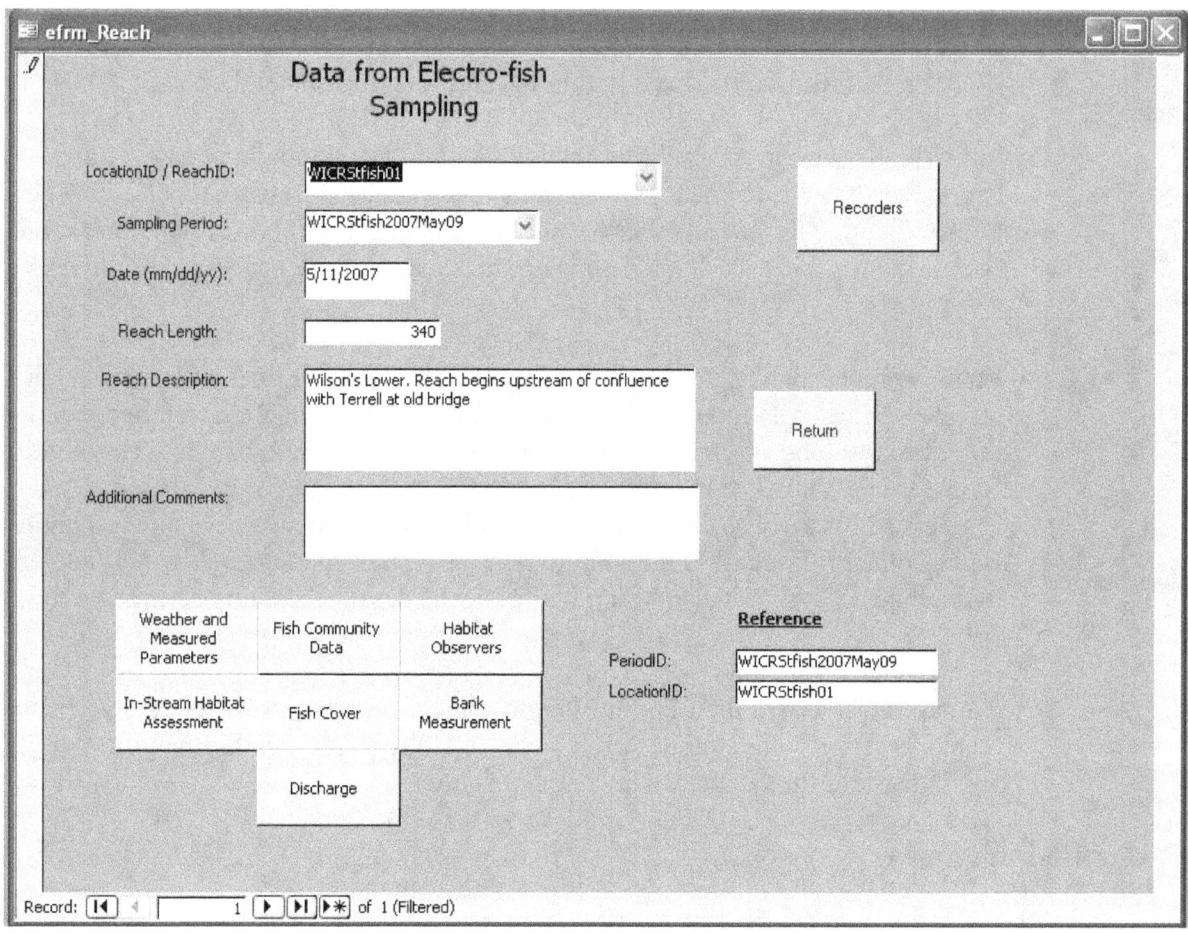

Figure 5. Main window for entering electro-fish data.

**Entering Weather and Reach Conditions**

Procedures:

1. In the main window (Figure 5), click on Weather and Measured Parameters.

2. Enter values for weather conditions including percent cloud cover, wind, and type and intensity of precipitation.

3. Return to the main electro-fish window.

**Entering Reach Habitat Data**

Entry of physical habitat data for a reach consists of four forms: Habitat Observers, In-stream Habitat Assessment, Fish Cover, and Bank Measurement.

Procedures:

1. Habitat Observers. In the main window (Figure 5), click on Habitat Observers, enter date spacing interval, and crew initials. Return to main electro-fish window.

2. In-stream Habitat Assessment. In the main window (Figure 5), click on In-stream Habitat Assessment button. Enter transect, channel, pool form, and width, and click on Enter Data button. Press enter to tab to transect location and enter transect location, depth, velocity, substrate, embeddedness, and canopy cover. Return to the main electro-fish window.

3. Fish Cover. In the main window (Figure 5), click on Fish Cover button and then the Fish Cover Data button. Using the return key, tab to transect and enter transect number, select transect location (left, center or right), and check off all fish cover types observed. Return to the main electro-fish window.

4. Bank Measurement. In the main window (Figure 5), click on Bank Measurement button and then on Bank Measurement Data button. Press enter to tab to the transect fields. Enter transect number and transect location (left or right), angle, vegetative cover, height, substrate, and bank cover types. Return to the main electro-fish window.

## Entering Discharge Data

Procedures:

1. In the main window (Figure 5), click on Discharge button. Set distance units, depth units, and velocity units, if different from default values.

2. Click on Enter Data button. Press enter to move to discharge number and enter discharge number, distance from bank, depth, velocity, and flag (additional comments). Return to the main electro-fish window.

## Entering Fish Community Data

Procedures:

1. In the main window (Figure 5), click on Fish Community Data.

2. Enter date, staff who identified fish and recorded data, the type of gear used, the sampling effort, and the habitat type.

3. Click on Crew Duties button. Select crew initials and select electro-fish duties. Return to Fish Community Data form.

4. Click on Fish Data button. Select a species for data entry and click on Add Individual Data button.

5. Individually weighed fish. Enter the total length, weight, and anomaly. If no anomalies exist, then enter "N". Indicate if the individual was kept as a voucher

(Yes/No) and enter the number of individuals (1, the default) and any comments for that fish.

6. Batch weighed fish. Enter the individual length, omit the weight, and enter a batch number and any anomalies for that individual. If all 30 fish are weighed together, then batch will be "1" for all fish of that species. If multiple batches are weighed for a species, then the first group is batch "1", the second group is batch "2", etc. The record for the last fish in the batch will have the batch weight entered under BatchTotalWt. Indicate if the individual was kept as a voucher (Yes/No) and enter the number of individuals (1, the default) and any comments for that fish.

7. Counted fish. Leave the Length, Weight, Batch, BatchTotalWt, and Age fields blank. Enter only the number of fish counted, any anomalies for the group of fish and indicate if the counted fish were vouchered

## Entering Water Quality Data

Water quality data will be collected by unattended CORE 5 data loggers (sondes) at all reaches at PIPE, HOME, EFMO, GWCA, HEHO, HOSP, PERI, WICR and at selected reaches at TAPR. These data are uploaded from the logger using the manufacturer's accompanying software program and saved in MS Excel. Data are then edited to correct any missing data due to logger maintenance (down time) and validated to determine if the data meet the expected range requirements or critical limits. CORE 5 water quality summary data are then entered into NPStoret either by using the direct data-entry templates or the import module. Metadata is then entered for each characteristic/parameter. Coordinate data for logger locations are collected in accordance with the current HTLN spatial data collection techniques and entered into NPStoret. An NPStoret database is then sent to the WRD staff on an annual basis for initial QA/QC and subsequent upload into the WRD master copy of the EPA STORET.

## IV. Data Verification

Data verification immediately follows data entry. Computer records are verified for accuracy against paper field data sheets. Hard copy of data records should be used in the verification against field data to minimize proof-reading error. Compare the output directly with original field data sheets to identify missing, mismatched, or redundant records. The verification step should be completed by staff other than those doing data entry, if possible, and by someone familiar with the project. Following verification, the project manager should recheck 10% of the records. The verification process should be repeated until no errors are discovered.

Procedures:

1. Print pertinent data and compare with original field forms

2. Reconcile errors in database

3. Recheck 10% of records. If errors are detected, repeat the entire process.

# V. Data Validation

Data validation involves checking the accuracy of data against outside controls or specifications. Four types of data validation are used with Stfish. They are:

- Referential integrity
- Limited lists for nominal data
- Reasonable values for continuous attribute data
- Reasonable coordinates for spatial data

Referential integrity and data validation for nominal data are typically built into the database and require little or no maintenance. Checking for reasonable values for continuous attribute data and spatial data requires the attention of the project manager and staff familiar with GIS. Knowledge of the sampling design and underlying ecological processes is necessary to identify extreme outliers that are not natural members of the distribution of measured ecological parameters.

## Referential Integrity

Referential integrity is a property of the relationships between database tables. You create referential integrity by imposing rules or constraints on the relationships between key fields. A key can be either a primary key or a foreign key depending upon what rules are assigned to it. Primary key values must be unique and cannot be null. Each value in a foreign key must be derived from the domain of its related primary key. Referential constraints prevent dangling references between rows of related tables (Roman, 2002). Further, they reduce the chance of inadvertent record deletions.

## Nominal data

Nominal data can be validated during the data-entry process by limiting data to specific pre-determined values in the data-entry forms. Examples of nominal data in Stfish include LocationID, PeriodID, Species, SiteID, stream flow, site substrate, and riparian classification values. Values should be chosen from lists or combo boxes to the greatest extent possible in the database forms. The forms typically require little or no maintenance.

## Continuous data

Validation of continuous data typically requires the attention of the project manager. Knowledge of the ecological system is necessary to determine what constitutes a reasonable quantitative value for a particular parameter. The data can be exported to a statistical package for quantitative validation.

Procedures:

1. Export the datasets of interest (see Exporting Data, below).

2. Import the data into a spreadsheet or statistical package.

3. Calculate descriptive statistics such as mean, median, standard deviation, range, and sample size. Plot a histogram and identify outlier values.

4. Extreme individual values may indicate recording or data-entry errors.

**Spatial Data**

Spatial validation of sample coordinates can be accomplished using the ArcMap component of ArcGIS. Spatial data are maintained in the project shape file(s) derived from GPS data. They can be added to an ArcMap project and compared with existing features (*i.e.*, park boundaries, USGS Digital Orthophoto Quarter Quadrangles, National Hydrography Dataset hydrography, *etc.*) to confirm that coordinate data are valid.

Procedures:

1. Develop testing project within ArcMap constrained to appropriate UTM zone and projection (14N or 15N, NAD83).

2. Add park unit boundaries and any necessary spatial data (roads, water, contour, *etc.*).

3. Add relevant site coordinate data to testing project and validate against known features.

4. Identify errors and determine their cause. Systematic bias may indicate incorrect mapping project settings in the GPS unit. Unusually large error may indicate limited availability of GPS satellites due to tree canopy or other physical structures, GPS operator error, or simply orientation issues during field work. Correction of GPS coordinate errors may require site revisits to maintain positional accuracy.

5. Develop metadata for final spatial dataset.

**VI. Exporting Data**

Monitoring data can be exported from Stfish and imported into software packages such as spreadsheets and statistical packages. Each export category follows the design shown in Figure 3. Export data sets are organized by park and year. This organization should facilitate comparison of the same parameters across multiple years and between multiple parameters within years.

Procedures:

1. Click on Export Seine Data from the switchboard.

2. Select year and park code.

3. Click on reach data to view all reach data available for the selected year and park.

4. The query results begin with the year and park code. This is true for each export query. In addition, LocationID, PeriodID, and EventID are provided where possible.

5. To export the data outside the database, select File -> Export from the menu bar. There are many options available for export format. These include spreadsheets, text files, and XML. Data connectivity via ODBC is also available to dynamically link to other database and GIS systems.

## VI. File Organization

The various databases, reports and GIS coverages used and generated by the Heartland Network create a large number of files and folders to manage. Poor file organization can lead to confusion and data corruption. As a standard data management technique, files pertaining to the project are managed in their own folder: Analysis, for data analysis; Data, for copies of archived data as well as data sheets; Documents, for supporting materials related to the project; and Spatial info, for various spatial data. The databases are managed in the Database folders and contain prior versions of the database in a subfolder. The use of standardized filesystems is especially critical where multiple parties require access to shared folders, files, and data sets. Standardized filesystems are also important to maintain tape back-up systems and program operations during periods of staff turnover.

## VII. Version Control

Prior to any major changes of a data set, a copy is stored with the appropriate version number. This allows for the tracking of changes over time. With proper controls and communication, versioning ensures that only the most current version is used in any analysis. Daily backups can be made using the Access backup feature (which creates a backup file with the date appended to the database name) during periods of active data entry. For archive backups that will be stored permanently, versioning of archived data sets is handled by adding a floating-point number to the file name, with the first version being numbered 1.0. Each major version is assigned a sequentially higher whole number. Each minor version is assigned a sequentially higher .1 number. Major version changes include migrations across Access versions and complete rebuilds of front-ends and analysis tools. Minor version changes include bug fixes in front-end and analysis tools. Frequent users of the data are notified of the updates, and provided with a copy of the most recent archived version.

## VIII. Backups

Secure data archiving is essential for protecting data files from corruption. Once a data set has passed the QA/QC procedures specified in the protocol, a new metadata record is created using the NPS Metadata Tools (stand alone or within ArcCatalog) or Dataset Catalog. Backup copies of the data are maintained at both on- and off-site locations. An additional digital copy is forwarded to the NPS I&M Data Store. Tape backups of all data are made at regular intervals in accordance with current HTLN backup standard operating procedures and will be made minimally, once per week, with semi-annual tapes permanently archived (see Rowell, 2007).

Procedures:

1. Create metadata record pursuant to data archiving.

2. Backup data.

3. Store backup copies on- and off-site and forward a copy to the I&M Data Store.

4. Administer regularly scheduled backups of data.


## IX. Data Availability

Currently, data are available for research and management applications for those database versions where all QA/QC has been completed and the data have been archived. Data can be transferred using ftp or by e-mail (where files are smaller than a few megabytes). Monitoring data will become generally available for download directly from the NPS I&M Data Store. Metadata for the small stream fish community database are developed using ESRI ArcCatalog 9.2 and the NPS Metadata Tools and Editor extension and will be available at the NPS I&M GIS server (http://science.nature.nps.gov/nrdata/). Water quality data will be stored at the EPA STORET National Data Warehouse (USEPA, 2007) and be publicly accessible via the Internet. Additionally, data requests can be directed to:

Data Manager
Heartland I&M Network
National Park Service
Wilson's Creek National Battlefield
6424 W. Farm Road 182
Republic MO 65738

## SOP 9: Data Analysis

## Version 1.00 (05/01/2008)

**Revision History Log:**

| Previous Version # | Revision Date | Author | Changes Made | Reason for Change | New Version # |
|---|---|---|---|---|---|
| | | | | | |
| | | | | | |
| | | | | | |
| | | | | | |
| | | | | | |

Ecological studies based on biological, chemical, and physical data are used by resource managers to better comprehend underlying system processes and develop environmental/management policies that best serve the resource. A critical component of any long-term monitoring protocol is a consistent and systematic approach to analyzing and reporting data. This information must describe the current condition, or status, of a community, and be robust enough to detect community changes through time. This, in turn, could have substantial ecological repercussions and should be an important consideration for investigators responsible for data interpretation. Therefore, every effort should be made to collect reliable data and use statistical analyses that are straightforward and will result in confident interpretations. This SOP describes the metrics to be calculated for fish and habitat data collected from small streams, and statistical analyses for interpreting those metrics.

## I. Metrics and Estimated Parameters for Fish Community and Habitat Analyses

Primary approaches to analyzing fish and habitat data will include metric/parameter estimation with use of control charts and multivariate statistics. Biological metrics are commonly used by investigators at all levels (*e.g.*, private, state, tribal, and federal) to compare the condition of the biological community at multiple sites (Simon, 1999) or examine trends across time. Barbour *et al.* (1999) define a metric as a characteristic of the biota that changes in an expected direction with increased anthropogenic disturbance. Using these characteristics (Table 2) allows investigators to determine the importance of environmental conditions, clarify which habitat factors play a large role in shaping fish communities, and identify specific sources of impairment (Karr, 1981).

By combining multiple metrics (and results for those metrics) into a single index of biotic integrity (IBI), investigators can determine the overall quality of the fish community. An IBI can also be used to compare overall ecological conditions over time and among sites, providing the selected metrics are related to variables responsible for impairment (Karr, 1981; Barbour *et al.*, 1999; Simon, 1999).

**Fish Metrics**

1. **Species Richness**. The number of species collected for the entire sample reach. Typically, species richness declines with increases in human disturbance.

2. **Simpson's Diversity Index**. This index uses both richness and abundance to calculate diversity of the fish community. This index is preferable to the Shannon diversity index and will be used for data analysis because this index is independent of sample size. This index decreases with poor water quality and habitat conditions. Simpson's Diversity Index is calculated with the formula shown below.

$$D = \sum((n^2 - n)/(N^2 - N))$$

n = number of individuals of *i*th species, and N = $\sum$n.

3. **Catch per Unit Effort**. Catch per unit effort (CPUE) can be calculated as either Catch per Time or Catch per Area sampled. When using electrofishing gear to collect community data, CPUE is typically calculated as Catch per Time. We will use catch per minute to obtain relative abundance. When using seining methods, CPUE is typically calculated as Catch per Area. We will use catch per square meter. Total CPUE will be calculated using the total number of fish collected at a reach. CPUE for each individual species will also be calculated at each reach.

4. **Size Structure**. Size structures of fish populations within the community can be indicative of a disturbance or resource problem. A community with primarily larger fish indicates that there is little recruitment to keep the community self-sustaining. A community with primarily smaller fish could indicate inadequate resources (*e.g.*, food resources) that limit growth. Average length and weight (and ranges) for each species at the reach will be calculated.

5. **Percent Composition**. Percent composition by biomass will be calculated for each species in the reach. To calculate this:

First, calculate individual biomass for each species ($B_i$):

$$B_i = W_i N_i$$

$W_i$ = average weight of fish species *i*
$N_i$ = number of individuals of species *i*

Second, calculate biomass per area for each species ($BPA_i$) and total biomass per area ($BPA_t$):

$$BPA_i = B_i / A$$

96

$$BPA_t = \sum BPA_i$$

A = area of the sample reach

Lastly, calculate percent composition for each species ($C_i$)

$$C_i = BPA_i / BPA_t * 100$$

## Index of Biotic Integrity

Several IBI's have been developed for various regions and states (Fausch *et al.*, 1984; Lyons *et al.*, 1996; Hlass *et al.*, 1998; Yoder and Smith, 1999; Dauwalter *et al.*, 2003; and Smogor, 2005). We will *evaluate* specific IBI's for use at parks located in regions or states that have a published IBI. Individual metrics are calculated and scored. Scores are totaled for an IBI score. The higher the IBI score the better the condition of the community.

1.  For those parks located in the Ozark Highlands, the IBI by Dauwalter *et al.* (2003) will be evaluated for use in streams at GWCA, PERI, and WICR. Details on calculation and scoring of metrics can be found in Dauwalter *et al.* (2003). The metrics used in this IBI are:

    a.  percent of individuals as algivorous/herbivorous, invertivorous, and piscivorous
    b.  percent of individuals with black spot or an anomaly
    c.  percent of individuals as green sunfish, bluegill, yellow bullhead, and channel catfish
    d.  percent of individuals as invertivorous
    e.  percent of individuals as top carnivores
    f.  number of darter, sculpin, and madtom species
    g.  number of lithophilic spawning species

2.  For HOSP, which is located in the Ouachita Mountains region, the IBI developed by Hlass *et al.* (1998) will be assessed for use in these streams. Details on calculation and scoring of metrics can be found in Hlass *et al.* (1998). Metrics in this IBI include:

    a.  Number of native species
    b.  Number of intolerant species
    c.  Number of minnow species
    d.  Proportion of individuals as green sunfish
    e.  Proportion of individuals as top carnivores
    f.  Ratio of generalist to specialist feeders
    g.  Number of individuals in sample (catch per minute)
    h.  Proportion of individuals with disease or other anomaly

3.  For the remaining parks, the IBI used by Fausch *et al.* (1984) in the Midwest region, will be evaluated for use in streams at EFMO, HEHO, HOME, PIPE, and TAPR. Metrics calculated in this IBI are:

a. Number of species
b. Number of darter species
c. Number of sunfish species
d. Number of sucker species
e. Number of intolerant species
f. Proportion of individuals as green sunfish
g. Proportion of individuals as omnivores
h. Proportion of individuals as insectivorous minnows
i. Proportion of individuals as top carnivores
j. Number of individuals in sample
k. Proportion of individuals as hybrids
l. Proportion of individuals with disease, tumors, fin damage, or other anomalies

## Habitat and Water Quality Parameters

Physical and chemical habitat measurements will be estimated using summary statistics such as means, medians, standard errors and/or confidence intervals. In the simplest presentation of data, each parameter should be estimated in each year that data are available, and confidence intervals or standard errors calculated, where appropriate. For parameters where percentage cover class categories are used (such as substrate, embeddedness, canopy cover) the median value of the cover class will be used in calculating means and standard errors. Those parameters where presence/absence data are collected (such as fish cover and bank cover types), a percentage will be calculated for the reach.

## II. Control Charts

The construction and interpretation of control charts is covered in many texts focusing on quality control in industry (*e.g.*, Beauregard *et al.*, 1992; Gyrna, 2001; Montgomery, 2001). The application of control charts for ecological purposes, however, is relatively straightforward and will be used for the interpretation of fish community data collected under this protocol. The use of control charts in environmental monitoring is discussed in texts by McBean and Rovers (1998) and Manly (2001), although not in as great detail as the texts referenced above focusing on industrial applications. Many different types of control charts could be constructed, depending upon the type of information desired. For example, control charts can be used to evaluate variables or attributes (*i.e.*, count or frequency data), focus on measures of central tendency or dispersion, and be used in univariate or multivariate analyses (Morrison 2008).

Most traditional control charts assume that observations come from a normal distribution, or that data can be transformed to normality. In industry, control limits are often set at a distance of 3 standard deviations on either side of the centerline (Wetherill and Brown, 1991; Beauregard *et al.*, 1992; Montgomery, 2001). Thus, assuming a normal distribution centered at the centerline, the control limits would encompass 99.73% of the distribution.

Control limits may be constructed so as to contain any desired proportion of the distribution (i.e., representing [1-$\alpha$] confidence intervals for any $\alpha$). In this case, choosing control limits is equivalent to specifying a critical region for testing the hypothesis that a specific observation is statistically different from the proposed centerline value. It is crucial that the centerline value is representative of the true population parameter. Control limits could also be based on probabilistic thresholds other than confidence intervals (*e.g.*, McBean and Rovers, 1998).

If the observations cannot be assumed to come from a normal distribution, there are several options available beyond simple transformations of data. One option is to create subgroups of consecutive samples, and then use the subgroup averages, which will be approximately normally distributed in accordance with the central limit theorem (see Beauregard *et al.*, 1992; Montgomery, 2001). It is possible to construct control charts based on other distributions (*e.g.*, a Poisson distribution as in Atkinson *et al.*, 2003), and construct analogous confidence limits, as long as the distributions are known. Distribution-free confidence limits may also be calculated, although these will usually be relatively wide and less sensitive to changes (Conover, 1999).

It is not absolutely necessary to use values from a statistical sampling process to determine centerlines and thresholds for action. One can also subjectively choose a centerline value as the desired state and set threshold limits to match an acceptable amount of variability for the variable of interest. It is crucial to realize that this approach has no statistical basis, and thus probabilities cannot be readily associated with the observations. This application also has a precedent in industry. Such charts, which plot observations without relevance to an underlying distribution, have been termed 'conformance charts'. Threshold values, which may be subjective, are termed 'action limits' (Beauregard *et al.*, 1992). If taking this approach, one should be very familiar with the system in question, and preferably select values that are defensible based on the data.

Although control charts have potentially wide applicability, each application may be different. A generic process for control chart construction is provided below, although decisions will always have to be made and an analyst familiar with control charts should ideally be consulted.

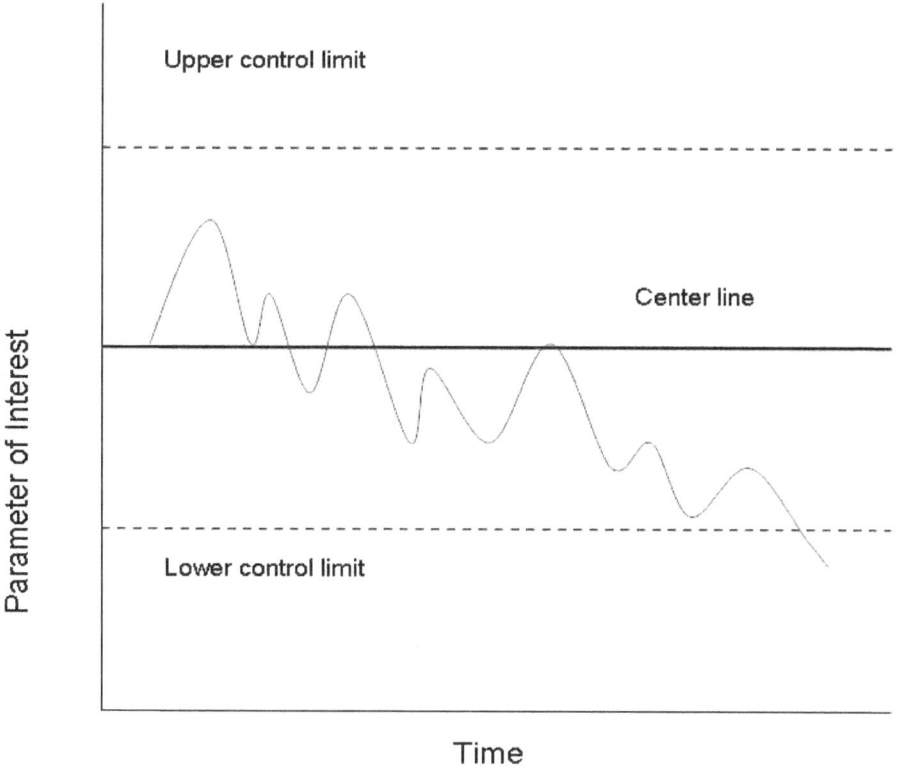

Figure 1. Generic univariate control chart.

Steps in constructing a univariate control chart (see Figure 1):

1. Determine the parameter of interest. This may be any of the metrics presented above.

2. After several data points are available, plot the values of the parameter of interest (on the y-axis) against time (on the x-axis).

3. Determined a "center-line" value for this parameter, which could represent a mean of the observations, a target value, or some other value. Determining an appropriate center-line contains inherent pitfalls, and an analyst who is familiar with control charts should be consulted.

4. Establish control limits around the center-line. It is possible that only an upper control limit, or only a lower control limit, or both will be necessary, depending upon the parameter of interest and management concerns. Control limits may be based on a probability distribution and thus allow one to make statistical inferences, or they may be based on target levels set by management. Once again, determining appropriate control limits can be tricky, especially if statistical inferences are desired, and an analyst who is familiar with control charts should be consulted.

5. Continue to plot values of the parameter of interest over time as new data become available. If an observation exceeds the control limit(s), this is indicative of the potential need for management action, or a more focused study.

Control charts should be constructed after several data points are available, and updated regularly. Additional control charts can be constructed from other variables of interest as described above.


## III. Other Methods

Multivariate analysis is another frequently used analysis technique and involves methods used to explain variability in community data and to identify the environmental variables that best explain, and have an assumed responsibility for, the variability measured (Gauch, 1982; Jongman et al., 1995; Everitt and Dunn, 2001; Timm, 2002). Multivariate techniques elicit a hypothesis from the biological data rather than disproving a null hypothesis. Two commonly used multivariate techniques include: ordination (such as principal components analysis, canonical correspondence analysis, and detrended correspondence analysis) and classification (such as two-way indicator species analysis). Detailed discussion of these methods can be found in several texts (Gauch, 1982; Jongman et al., 1995; Everitt and Dunn, 2001; Timm, 2002).

If a hypothesis testing approach is deemed appropriate, many tests may be employed, depending upon the question being asked and the structure of the data. For example, a Kruskal-Wallace ANOVA may be used to test for significant differences among sites within seined reaches. If there is reason to compare more than two variables among samples, Friedman's non-parametric two-way analysis of variance should be used.

Table 2. Fish species classifications by tolerance, trophic status, spawning preference, and federal and state status. For federal status, E = endangered, T = threatened, and C = candidate. State status is divided into threatened and endangered (T&E) and species of concern (SC). States are abbreviated as AR = Arkansas, IA = Iowa, KS = Kansas, MN = Minnesota, MO = Missouri, and NE = Nebraska.

| Common Name | Scientific Name | Lithophilic Spawner | Top Feeder | Diet | Tolerance | Federal Status | State T&E | State SC |
|---|---|---|---|---|---|---|---|---|
| Alabama shad | Alosa alabamae | | | Piscivorous | Moderate | | | AR, MO |
| Alligator gar | Lepisosteus spatula | | X | Piscivorous | Moderate | | | AR, |
| American brook lamprey | Lampetra appendix | X | | Filter feeder | Intolerant | | IA | AR,IA,MO |
| American eel | Anguilla rostrata | | X | Piscivorous | Moderate | | | |
| Arkansas darter | Etheostoma cragini | X | | Invertivorous | Intolerant | C | KS | AR,KS,MO |
| Arkansas saddled darter | Etheostoma euzonum | X | | Insectivorous | Intolerant | | | MO |
| Banded darter | Etheostoma zonale | | | Insectivorous | Intolerant | | | KS |
| Banded sculpin | Cottus carolinae | X | | Insectivorous | Intolerant | | | KS |
| Bantam sunfish | Lepomis symmetricus | X | Inse | ctivorous | Moderate | | | MO |
| Bigeye chub | Notropis amblops | X | | Insectivorous | Intolerant | | | |
| Bigeye shiner | Notropis boops | X | | Insectivorous | Intolerant | | | |
| Bigmouth buffalo | Ictiobus cyprinellus | | | Insectivorous | Moderate | | | |
| Bigmouth shiner | Notropis dorsalis | X | | Insectivorous | Moderate | | | |
| Black buffalo | Ictiobus niger | | | Insectivorous | Moderate | | | NE |
| Black bullhead | Ameiurus melas | X | | Insectivorous | Moderate | | | |
| Black crappie | Pomoxis nigromaculatus | | X | Piscivorous | Moderate | | | |
| Black redhorse | Moxostoma duquesnei | X | | Insectivorous | Intolerant | | IA | IA,KS |
| Black River madtom | Noturus maydeni | X | | Insectivorous | Intolerant | | | |
| Blacknose dace | Rhinichthys atratulus | X | | Generalist | Tolerant | | | KS,NE |
| Blacknose shiner | Notropis heterolepis | X | | Insectivorous | Intolerant | | IA,NE | IA,MO,NE |
| Blackside darter | Percina maculata | X | | Insectivorous | Moderate | | KS,NE | KS,NE |
| Blackspotted topminnow | Fundulus olivaceus | | | Insectivorous | Moderate | | | |
| Blackstripe topminnow | Fundulus notatus | | | Insectivorous | Moderate | | | |
| Blacktail shiner | Cyprinella venusta | | | Insectivorous | Moderate | | | |
| Bleeding shiner | Luxilus zonatus | X | | Invertivorous | Moderate | | | |
| Blue catfish | Ictalurus furcatus | | | Piscivorous | Moderate | | | |
| Blue sucker | Cycleptus elongatus | X | | Insectivorous | Intolerant | | | KS,MN,MO,NE |
| Blue breast darter | Etheostoma camurum | X | | Insectivorous | Intolerant | | | |
| Bluegill | Lepomis macrochirus | | | Insectivorous | Tolerant | | | |

| Common name | Scientific name | | Trophic guild | Tolerance | | |
|---|---|---|---|---|---|---|
| Bluestripe darter | Percina cymatotaenia | X | Insectivorous | Moderate | | MO |
| Bluntface shiner | Cyprinella camura | | Insectivorous | Intolerant | | MO |
| Bluntnose darter | Etheostoma chlorosomum | | Insectivorous | Moderate | IA | IA,KS |
| Bluntnose minnow | Pimephales notatus | | Omnivore | Tolerant | | NE |
| Bowfin | Amia calva | X | Piscivorous | Moderate | | |
| Brassy minnow | Hybognathus hankinsoni | | Omnivore | Moderate | | KS,MO |
| Brindled madtom | Noturus miurus | X | Insectivorous | Intolerant | | KS |
| Brook silverside | Labidesthes sicculus | | Insectivorous | Moderate | | |
| Brook stickleback | Culaea inconstans | | Insectivorous | Moderate | | NE |
| Brook trout | Salvelinus fontinalis | X | Piscivorous | Moderate | | |
| Brown bullhead | Ameiurus nebulosus | X | Insectivorous | Tolerant | | MO |
| Brown trout | Salmo trutta | X | Piscivorous | Intolerant | | |
| Bullhead minnow | Pimephales vigilax | | Omnivore | Moderate | | |
| Burbot | Lota lota | X | Piscivorous | Moderate | IA | IA |
| Cardinal shiner | Luxilus cardinalis | X | Generalist | Intolerant | | |
| Carmine shiner | Notropis percobromus | X | Insectivorous | Intolerant | | MO |
| Central mudminnow | Umbra limi | | Insectivorous | Tolerant | MO | |
| Central stoneroller | Campostoma anomalum | X | Algivorous | Moderate | | |
| Chain pickerel | Esox niger | X | Piscivorous | Moderate | | |
| Channel catfish | Ictalurus punctatus | | Piscivorous | Moderate | | |
| Channel darter | Percina copelandi | X | Insectivorous | Intolerant | | MO |
| Checkered madtom | Noturus flavater | X | Insectivorous | Intolerant | | MO |
| Chestnut lamprey | Ichthyomyzon castaneus | X | Piscivorous | Moderate | IA,KS | KS,NE |
| Common carp | Cyprinus carpio | | Omnivore | Tolerant | | |
| Common shiner | Luxilus cornutus | X | Insectivorous | Moderate | | NE |
| Creek chub | Semotilus atromaculatus | X | Generalist | Tolerant | | |
| Creek chubsucker | Erimyzon oblongus | X | Insectivorous | Moderate | | |
| Creole darter | Etheostoma collettei | X | Invertivorous | Moderate | | |
| Crystal darter | Crystallaria asprella | X | Insectivorous | Intolerant | MO | AR,MN,MO |
| Current River darter | Etheostoma uniporum | X | Insectivorous | Moderate | | |
| Current River saddled darter | Etheostoma euzonum erizonum | X | Insectivorous | Intolerant | | MO |
| Cutthroat trout | Oncorhynchus clarkii | X | Insectivorous | Intolerant | | |
| Cypress darter | Etheostoma proeliare | | Invertivorous | Moderate | | |
| Cypress minnow | Hybognathus hayi | | Herbivorous | Moderate | MO | MO |

102

| Common name | Scientific name | | Feeding | Tolerance | | |
|---|---|---|---|---|---|---|
| Dollar sunfish | Lepomis marginatus | X | Generalist | Moderate | | |
| Dusky darter | Percina sciera | X | Insectivorous | Moderate | | |
| Duskystripe shiner | Luxilus pilsbryi | X | Insectivorous | Intolerant | | |
| Eastern sand darter | Ammocrypta pellucida | X | Insectivorous | Intolerant | | |
| Emerald shiner | Notropis atherinoides | X | Insectivorous | Moderate | | |
| Fantail darter | Etheostoma flabellare | X | Insectivorous | Intolerant | | |
| Fathead minnow | Pimephales promelas | | Omnivore | Tolerant | | |
| Finescale dace | Phoxinus neogaeus | Inse | ctivorous | Moderate | NE | NE |
| Flathead catfish | Pylodictis olivaris | X | Piscivorous | Moderate | | |
| Flier | Centrarchus macropterus | X | Insectivorous | Moderate | | MO |
| Freckled madtom | Noturus nocturnus | X | Insectivorous | Moderate | IA | IA |
| Freshwater drum | Aplodinotus grunniens | | Invertivorous | Moderate | | |
| Ghost shiner | Notropis buchanani | X | Insectivorous | Moderate | | MO |
| Gilt darter | Percina evides | X | Insectivorous | Intolerant | | MN |
| Gizzard shad | Dorosoma cepedianum | | Omnivore | Tolerant | | |
| Golden redhorse | Moxostoma erythrurum | X | Insectivorous | Moderate | | |
| Golden shiner | Notemigonus crysoleucas | | Omnivore | Tolerant | | |
| Golden topminnow | Fundulus chrysotus | | Insectivorous | Intolerant | | MO |
| Goldeye | Hiodon alosoides | X | Insectivorous | Intolerant | | |
| Goldfish | Carassius auratus | | Omnivore | Tolerant | | |
| Grass carp | Ctenopharyngodon idella | | Herbivorous | Moderate | | |
| Grass pickerel | Esox americanus | X | Piscivorous | Moderate | IA | IA |
| Gravel chub | Erimystax x-punctatus | X | Insectivorous | Intolerant | | KS,MN |
| Greater redhorse | Moxostoma valenciennesi | X | Insectivorous | Intolerant | | |
| Green sunfish | Lepomis cyanellus | | Invertivorous | Tolerant | | |
| Greenside darter | Etheostoma blennioides | | Insectivorous | Intolerant | | KS |
| Harlequin darter | Etheostoma histrio | X | Insectivorous | Intolerant | | MO |
| Highfin carpsucker | Carpiodes velifer | | Omnivore | Intolerant | MO | KS,MO,NE |
| Hornyhead chub | Nocomis biguttatus | X | Insectivorous | Intolerant | KS | KS |
| Inland silverside | Menidia beryllina | | Insectivorous | Moderate | | |
| Iowa darter | Etheostoma exile | | Insectivorous | Moderate | | NE |
| Ironcolor shiner | Notropis chalybaeus | X | Insectivorous | Intolerant | | MO |
| Johnny darter | Etheostoma nigrum | X | Insectivorous | Moderate | | NE |
| Lake chubsucker | Erimyzon sucetta | X | Insectivorous | Moderate | | MO |
| Largemouth bass | Micropterus salmoides | X | Piscivorous | Tolerant | | |

| Common name | Scientific name | | | Trophic guild | Tolerance | | | |
|---|---|---|---|---|---|---|---|---|
| Largescale stoneroller | Campostoma oligolepis | X | | Algivorous | Moderate | | | AR |
| Least brook lamprey | Lampetra aepyptera | X | | Filter feeder | Moderate | | | |
| Logperch | Percina caprodes | X | | Insectivorous | Moderate | | | |
| Longear sunfish | Lepomis megalotis | X | | Insectivorous | Moderate | | | |
| Longnose dace | Rhinichthys cataractae | X | | Insectivorous | Intolerant | | | |
| Longnose gar | Lepisosteus osseus | | X | Piscivorous | Moderate | | | |
| Mimic shiner | Notropis volucellus | | | Insectivorous | Intolerant | | | MO |
| Mississippi silvery minnow | Hybognathus nuchalis | | | Herbivorous | Moderate | | | |
| Missouri saddled darter | Etheostoma tetrazonum | X | | Insectivorous | Intolerant | | | |
| Mooneye | Hiodon tergisus | | | Insectivorous | Intolerant | | | MO |
| Mosquitofish | Gambusia affinis | | | Insectivorous | Tolerant | | | |
| Mottled sculpin | Cottus bairdii | X | | Insectivorous | Intolerant | | | |
| Mud darter | Etheostoma asprigene | | | Insectivorous | Moderate | | | |
| Muskellunge | Esox masquinongy | | X | Piscivorous | Moderate | | | |
| Neosho madtom | Noturus placidus | X | | Insectivorous | Intolerant | T | KS,MO | KS,MO |
| Northern brook lamprey | Ichthyomyzon fossor | X | | Filter feeder | Intolerant | | | MN |
| Northern hog sucker | Hypentelium nigricans | X | | Insectivorous | Intolerant | | | KS |
| Northern pike | Esox lucius | | X | Piscivorous | Moderate | | | |
| Northern redbelly dace | Phoxinus eos | | | Herbivorous | Moderate | | NE | NE |
| Northern starhead | Fundulus dispar | | | Insectivorous | Intolerant | | | |
| Northern studfish | Fundulus catenatus | X | | Insectivorous | Intolerant | | | |
| Orangebelly darter | Etheostoma radiosum | X | | Invertivorous | Intolerant | | | |
| Orangespotted sunfish | Lepomis humilis | | | Insectivorous | Moderate | | | |
| Orangethroat darter | Etheostoma spectabile | X | | Insectivorous | Moderate | | IA | IA,NE |
| Ouachita madtom | Noturus lachneri | X | | Invertivorous | Intolerant | | | AR |
| Ozark bass | Ambloplites constellatus | | X | Piscivorous | Intolerant | | | AR |
| Ozark chub | Erimystax harryi | X | | Insectivorous | Moderate | | | |
| Ozark madtom | Noturus albater | X | | Insectivorous | Intolerant | | | |
| Ozark minnow | Notropis nubilus | X | | Herbivorous | Intolerant | | | KS,MN |
| Ozark sculpin | Cottus hypselurus | X | | Insectivorous | Intolerant | | | |
| Ozark shiner | Notropis ozarcanus | X | | Herbivorous | Intolerant | | | |
| Paddlefish | Polyodon spathula | X | | Filter feeder | Moderate | | | MO |
| Pallid shiner | Notropis amnis | X | | Insectivorous | Intolerant | | MN | AR,MN,MO,NE |
| Pirate perch | Aphredoderus sayanus | | | Insectivorous | Moderate | | | MN,MO |
| Plains topminnow | Fundulus sciadicus | | | Insectivorous | Intolerant | | | MO,MN,NE |

104

| Common name | Scientific name | | Trophic | Tolerance | | |
|---|---|---|---|---|---|---|
| Pugnose minnow | Opsopoeodus emiliae | X | Insectivorous | Intolerant | | IA |
| Pumpkinseed | Lepomis gibbosus | | Insectivorous | Moderate | | |
| Quillback | Carpiodes cyprinus | | Omnivore | Moderate | | |
| Rainbow darter | Etheostoma caeruleum | X | Insectivorous | Moderate | | |
| Rainbow trout | Oncorhynchus mykiss | X | Piscivorous | Intolerant | | |
| Red shiner | Cyprinella lutrensis | X | Insectivorous | Moderate | | |
| Redear sunfish | Lepomis microlophus | | Insectivorous | Moderate | | |
| Redfin shiner | Lythrurus umbratilis | X | Insectivorous | Moderate | | |
| Redhorse spp. | Moxostoma sp. | X | Insectivorous | Moderate | | |
| Redside dace | Clinostomus elongatus | X | Insectivorous | Intolerant | | |
| Redspot chub | Nocomis asper | X | Insectivorous | Intolerant | KS | KS |
| Redspotted sunfish | Lepomis miniatus | | Insectivorous | Moderate | | |
| Ribbon shiner | Lythrurus fumeus | X | Insectivorous | Moderate | | |
| River carpsucker | Carpiodes carpio | | Omnivore | Moderate | | |
| River chub | Nocomis micropogon | X | Insectivorous | Intolerant | | |
| River darter | Percina shumardi | X | Insectivorous | Moderate | | KS,MO |
| River redhorse | Moxostoma carinatum | X | Insectivorous | Intolerant | | KS |
| River shiner | Notropis blennius | X | Insectivorous | Moderate | | KS |
| Rock bass | Ambloplites rupestris | X | Piscivorous | Intolerant | | |
| Rosefin shiner | Lythrurus ardens | X | Insectivorous | Moderate | | |
| Sabine shiner | Notropis sabinae | X | Insectivorous | Moderate | | MO |
| Sand shiner | Notropis stramineus | X | Insectivorous | Moderate | | |
| Sauger Stizostedi | on canadense | X | Piscivorous | Moderate | | |
| Shadow bass | Ambloplites ariommus | X | Invertivorous | Intolerant | | |
| Shorthead redhorse | Moxostoma macrolepidotum | X | Insectivorous | Moderate | | |
| Shortnose gar | Lepisosteus platostomus | X | Piscivorous | Moderate | | |
| Shovelnose sturgeon | Scaphirhynchus platorynchus | X | Insectivorous | Moderate | MO | MO |
| Silver carp | Hypophthalmichthys molitrix | | Omnivore | Tolerant | | |
| Silver chub | Macrhybopsis storeriana | | Insectivorous | Moderate | KS | KS,MO |
| Silver lamprey | Ichthyomyzon unicuspis | X | Piscivorous | Moderate | | NE |
| Silver redhorse | Moxostoma anisurum | X | Insectivorous | Moderate | | AR |
| Silver shiner | Notropis photogenis | X | Insectivorous | Intolerant | | |
| Silverjaw minnow | Notropis buccatus | X | Insectivorous | Moderate | | |

| Common Name | Scientific Name | | Trophic Guild | Tolerance | | | |
|---|---|---|---|---|---|---|---|
| Skipjack herring | Alosa chrysochloris | X | Piscivorous | Moderate | | | MN |
| Slender madtom | Noturus exilis | | Insectivorous | Intolerant | X | | MN |
| Slenderhead darter | Percina phoxocephala | | Insectivorous | Intolerant | X | | AR |
| Slim minnow | Pimephales tenellus | | Insectivorous | Intolerant | X | | MO |
| Slough darter | Etheostoma gracile | | Insectivorous | Moderate | | | KS |
| Smallmouth bass | Micropterus dolomieu | X | Piscivorous | Intolerant | X | | |
| Smallmouth buffalo | Ictiobus bubalus | | Insectivorous | Moderate | | | |
| Southern cavefish | Typhlichthys subterraneus | | Invertivorous | Intolerant | | | AR,MO |
| Southern redbelly dace | Phoxinus erythrogaster | | Herbivorous | Intolerant | X | | |
| Speckled chub | Macrhybopsis aestivalis | | Insectivorous | Intolerant | | | |
| Speckled darter | Etheostoma stigmaeum | | Insectivorous | Intolerant | X | | KS |
| Spotfin shiner | Cyprinella spiloptera | | Insectivorous | Moderate | | | KS |
| Spottail shiner | Notropis hudsonius | | Insectivorous | Moderate | | | |
| Spotted bass | Micropterus punctulatus | X | Piscivorous | Moderate | | | |
| Spotted gar | Lepisosteus oculatus | X | Piscivorous | Moderate | | | |
| Spotted sucker | Minytrema melanops | | Insectivorous | Moderate | X | | KS |
| Spotted sunfish | Lepomis punctatus | | Insectivorous | Moderate | | | |
| Stargazing darter | Percina uranidea | | Insectivorous | Intolerant | X | | MO |
| Steelcolor shiner | Cyprinella whipplei | | Insectivorous | Intolerant | | | |
| Stippled darter | Etheostoma punctulatum | | Invertivorous | Intolerant | X | | KS |
| Stonecat | Noturus flavus | | Insectivorous | Intolerant | X | | |
| Stoneroller spp. | Campostoma spp. | | Algivorous | Moderate | X | | |
| Streamline chub | Erimystax dissimilis | | Insectivorous | Intolerant | X | | |
| Striped bass | Morone saxatilis | X | Insectivorous / Piscivorous | Moderate | | | |
| Striped mullet | Mugil cephalus | | Invertivorous | Moderate | | | |
| Striped shiner | Luxilus chrysocephalus | | Insectivorous | Moderate | X | | |
| Suckermouth minnow | Phenacobius mirabilis | | Insectivorous | Moderate | X | | |
| Swamp darter | Etheostoma fusiforme | | Insectivorous | Moderate | | MO | MO |
| Tadpole madtom | Noturus gyrinus | | Insectivorous | Moderate | X | | KS |
| Taillight shiner | Notropis maculatus | | Insectivorous | Moderate | | MO | MO |
| Telescope shiner | Notropis telescopus | | Insectivorous | Intolerant | X | | |
| Tippecanoe darter | Etheostoma tippecanoe | | Insectivorous | Intolerant | X | | |
| Topeka shiner | Notropis topeka | | Insectivorous | Intolerant E | X | IA,KS,MO,NE | IA,KS,MN,MO,NE |
| Treadfin shad | Dorosoma petenense | | Omnivore | Moderate | | | |
| Variegate darter | Etheostoma variatum | | Insectivorous | Intolerant | X | | |

| Common name | Species | | | Diet | Tolerance | | |
|---|---|---|---|---|---|---|---|
| Walleye Stizostedi | on vitreum | X | X | Piscivorous | Intolerant | | |
| Warmouth | Lepomis gulosus | | | Piscivorous | Moderate | | |
| Wedgespot shiner | Notropis greenei | X | | Insectivorous | Intolerant | | |
| Weed shiner | Notropis texanus | X | | Insectivorous | Intolerant | IA | IA,MO |
| Western sand darter | Ammocrypta clara | X | | Insectivorous | Intolerant | | MO |
| White bass | Morone chrysops | | X | Piscivorous | Moderate | | |
| White crappie | Pomoxis annularis | | X | Piscivorous | Moderate | | |
| White perch | Morone americana | | X | Piscivorous | Moderate | | |
| White sucker | Catostomus commersoni | X | | Omnivore | Tolerant | | |
| Whitetail shiner | Cyprinella galactura | | | Insectivorous | Intolerant | | |
| Yellow bass | Morone mississippiensis | | X | Piscivorous | Moderate | | MN |
| Yellow bullhead | Ameiurus natalis | X | | Insectivorous | Tolerant | | |
| Yellow perch | Perca flavescens | | X | Piscivorous | Moderate | | |
| Yoke darter | Etheostoma juliae | X | | Insectivorous | Intolerant | | |

107

**Protocol for Monitoring Fish Communities in Small Streams in the Heartland Inventory and Monitoring Network**

**SOP 10: Data Reporting**

**Version 1.00 (05/01/2008)**

**Revision History Log:**

| Previous Version # | Revision Date | Author | Changes Made | Reason for Change | New Version # |
|---|---|---|---|---|---|
|  |  |  |  |  |  |
|  |  |  |  |  |  |
|  |  |  |  |  |  |
|  |  |  |  |  |  |
|  |  |  |  |  |  |

This SOP gives instructions for reporting on fish community data and associated stream habitat and water quality collected at small streams in the Heartland Network. The SOP describes the procedure for formatting a report, the review process, and distribution of completed reports. Efficient reporting of monitoring results is critical in assisting park Resource Managers in management decisions.

**I. Report Format**

Template

The report template for regional natural resource technical reports should be followed (http://www.nature.nps.gov/publications/NRPM/index.cfm). Natural resource reports are the designated medium for disseminating high priority, current natural resource management information with managerial application. The natural resource technical reports series is used to disseminate the results of scientific studies in the physical, biological, and social sciences for both the advancement of science and the achievement of the National Park Service mission.

Style

Standards for scientific writing as recommended in the CBE Style Manual (1994) should be followed. Reports should be direct and concise. Refer to CBE Style Manual (1994), Mack (1986), Goldwasser (1999), Strunk and White (1999), and Day and Gastel (2006).

## II. Types of Reports and Review Procedure

Table 1. Summary of types of reports produced and review process. Adapted from DeBacker *et al.* (2005).

| Type of Report | Purpose of Report | Primary Audience | Review Process | Frequency |
|---|---|---|---|---|
| Annual Status Reports for Specific Protocols | Summarize monitoring data collected during the year and provide an update on the status of selected natural resources. Document related data management activities and data summaries. | Park resource managers and external scientists | Internal peer review by HTLN staff | Annually or every 3 years for parks on rotation |
| Executive Summary of Annual Reports for Specific Protocols | Same as Annual Status Reports but summarized to highlight key points for non-technical audiences. | Superintendents, interpreters, and the general public | Internal peer review by HTLN staff | Simultaneous with Annual Status Reports |
| Comprehensive Trends and Analysis and Synthesis Reports | Describe and interpret trends in individual vital signs. Describe and interpret relationships among observed trends and park management, known stressors, climate, *etc.* Highlight resources of concern that may require management action. | Park resource managers and external scientists | Internal peer review by HTLN staff | Every 5-10 years for annual parks or every 9 – 12 years for parks on rotation |
| Executive Summary of Comprehensive Trends and Analysis and Synthesis Reports | Same as Comprehensive Trends and Analysis and Synthesis Reports, but summarized to highlight findings and recommendations for non-technical audiences. | Superintendents, interpreters, and the general public | Internal peer review by HTLN staff | Simultaneous with Comprehensive Trends Analysis and Synthesis Reports |

### III. Distribution Procedure

Annual reports will be provided to the Resource Management staff and the Superintendent of each park. Additionally, a copy will be kept on file with the HTLN office of the National Park Service, Republic, Missouri. With the exception of reports that contain data on federally threatened and endangered species, reports will be made available to all interested parties upon request and posted on the HTLN website (http://science.nature.nps.gov/im/units/htln/). Data collected by the HTLN is public property and subject to requests under the Freedom of Information Act (FOIA).

**SOP 11:  Revising the Protocol**

**Version 1.00 (05/01/2008)**

## Revision History Log:

| Previous Version # | Revision Date | Author | Changes Made | Reason for Change | New Version # |
|---|---|---|---|---|---|
|  |  |  |  |  |  |
|  |  |  |  |  |  |
|  |  |  |  |  |  |
|  |  |  |  |  |  |
|  |  |  |  |  |  |

This SOP explains how to make changes to the Small Streams Fish Monitoring Protocol Narrative and accompanying SOPs and how to track these changes. Anyone asked to edit the Protocol Narrative or SOPs must follow this procedure to eliminate confusion in how data is collected and analyzed.

Procedures:

1. The Small Streams Fish Monitoring Protocol has used sound methodologies for collecting and analyzing data. All protocols require editing as new and different information becomes available. Required edits should be made in a timely manner and appropriate reviews undertaken.

2. All edits require review for clarity and technical soundness. Small changes or additions to existing methods will be reviewed in-house by the HTLN staff. However, if a complete change in methods is sought, then an outside review is required. Regional and national staff of the National Park Service with familiarity in fish community research and data analysis will be utilized as reviewers. Also, experts in fish community research and statistical methodologies outside of the Park Service will be used in the review process.

3. Document edits and protocol versioning in the Revision History Log that accompanies the Protocol Narrative and each SOP. Log changes in the Protocol Narrative or SOP being edited. Version numbers increase incrementally by hundredths (*e.g.*, version 1.01, version 1.02, ...*etc.*) for minor changes. Major revisions should be designated with the next whole number (*e.g.*, version 2.0, 3.0, 4.0 ...*etc.*). Record the previous version number, date of

revision, author of the revision, identify paragraphs and pages where changes are made, and the reason for making the changes along with the new version number.

4. Inform the Data Manager about changes to the Protocol Narrative or SOP so the new version number can be incorporated in the Metadata of the project database. The database may have to be edited by the Data Manager to accompany changes in the Protocol Narrative and SOPs.

5. Post new versions of the protocol on the Heartland Network internet website and forward copies to all individuals with a previous version of the affected Protocol Narrative or SOP.

Appendix A. Park maps with reach locations for sampling fish communities in small streams.

Figure 1. Map of historical reaches being retained (yellow) in this protocol and reaches being removed (red) from monitoring on Pipestone Creek, PIPE.

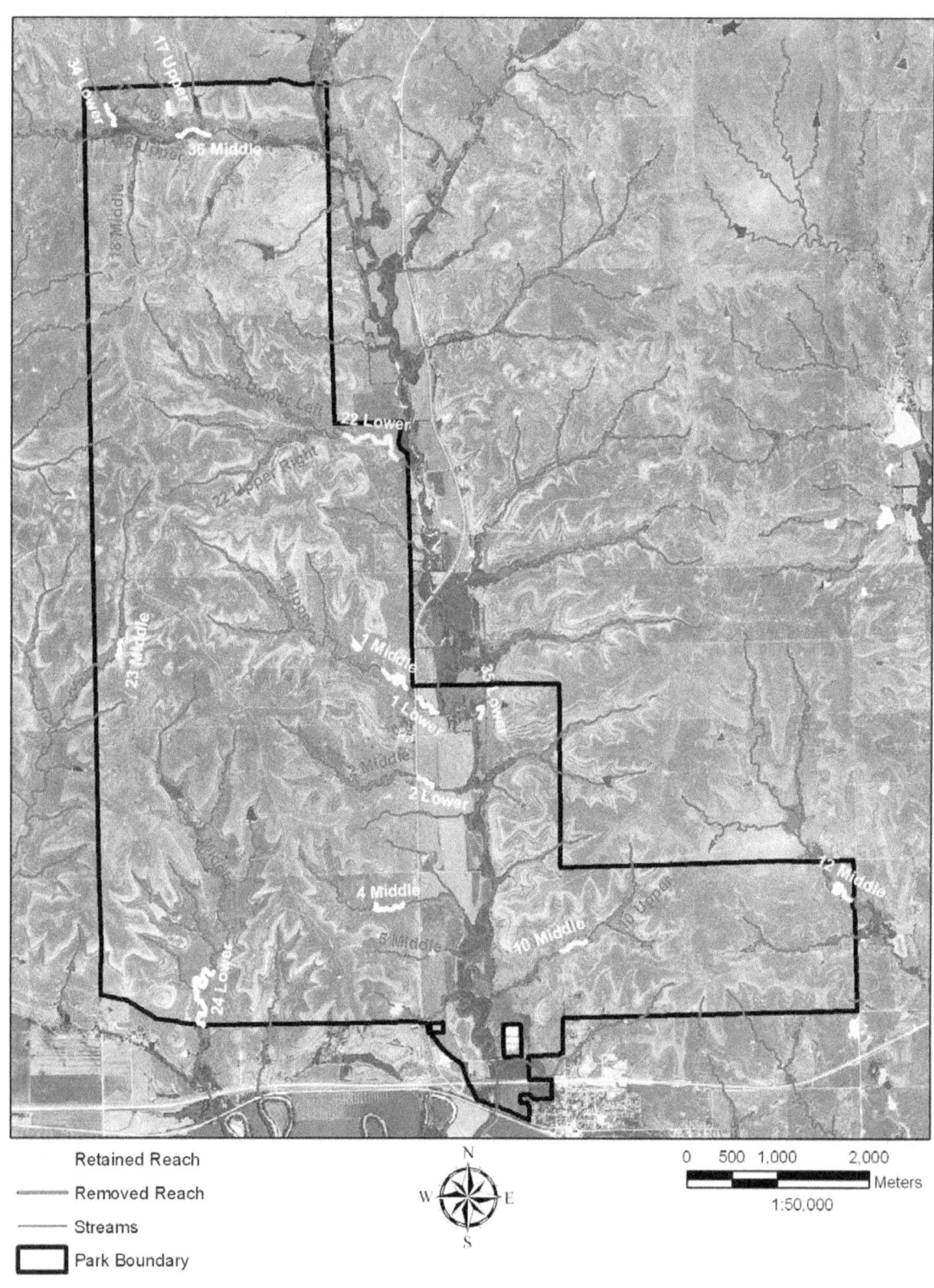

Figure 2. Map of historical reaches being retained (yellow) in this protocol and reaches being removed (red) from monitoring at TAPR.

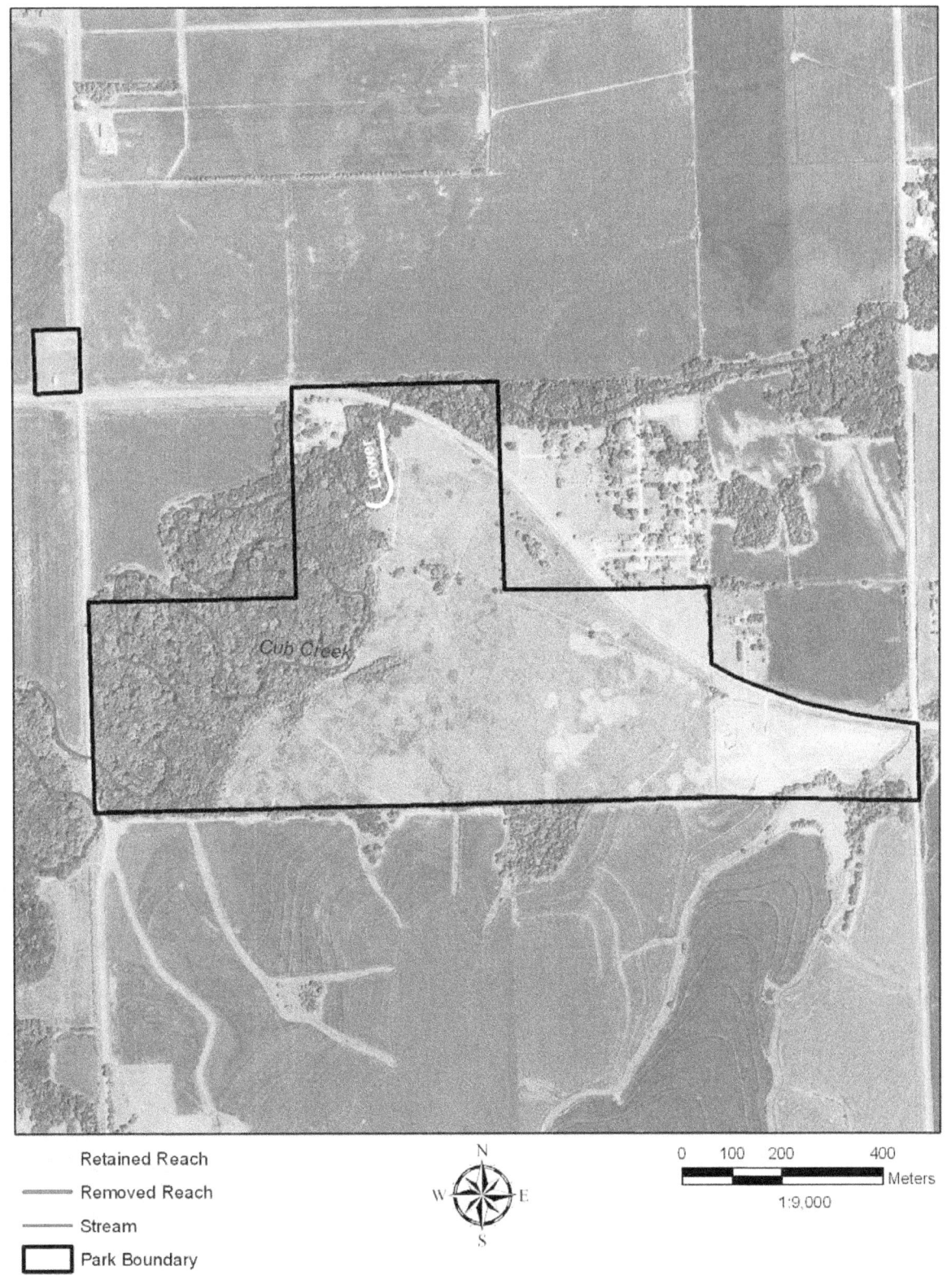

Retained Reach
Removed Reach
Stream
Park Boundary

Figure 3. Map of historical reach being retained (yellow) in this protocol and reach being removed (red) from monitoring on Cub Creek, HOME.

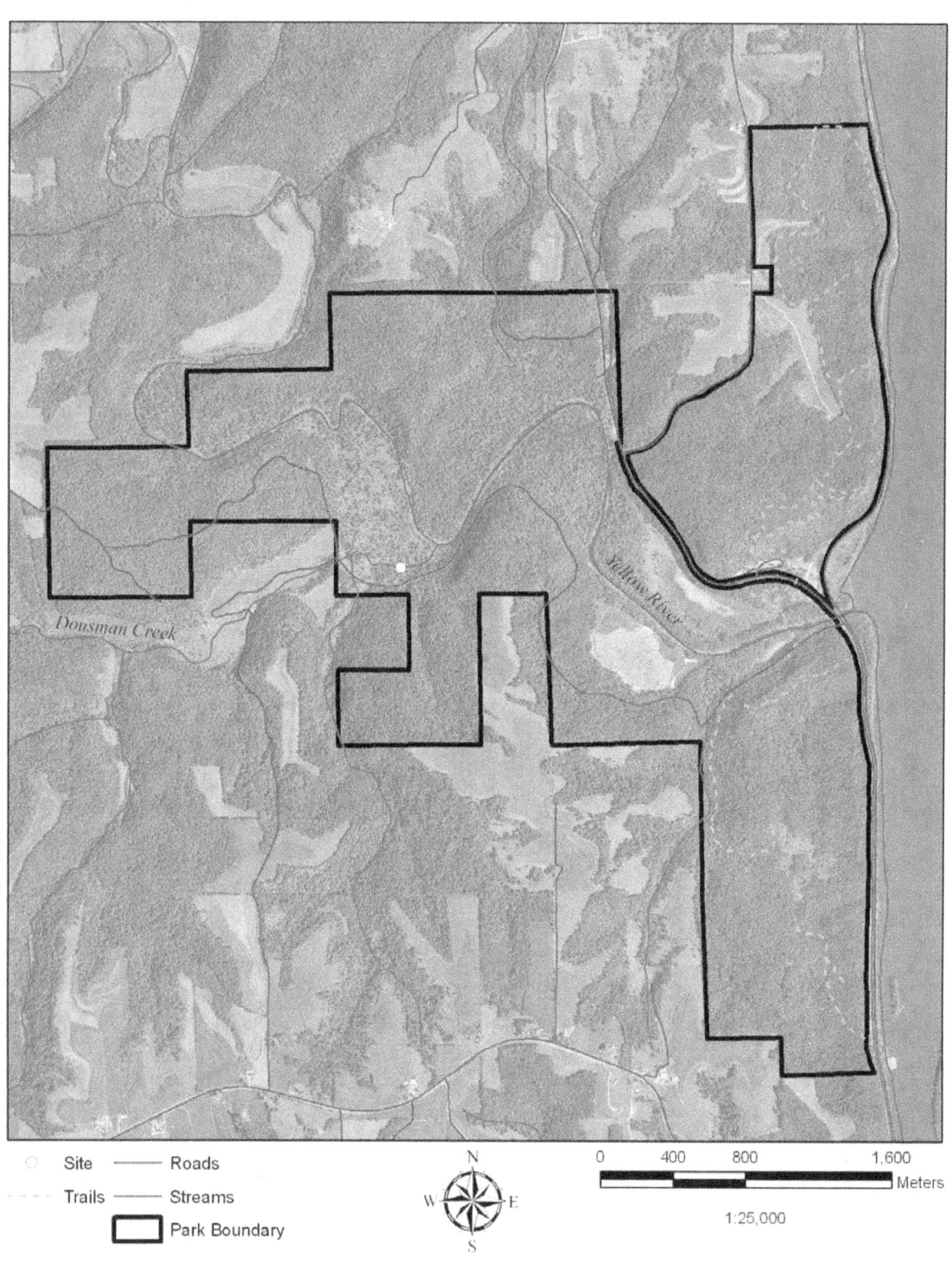

Figure 4. Map of sample site on Dousman Creek, EFMO.

Figure 5. Map of sample sites on Carver Creek, Harkins Branch, and Williams Branch, GWCA.

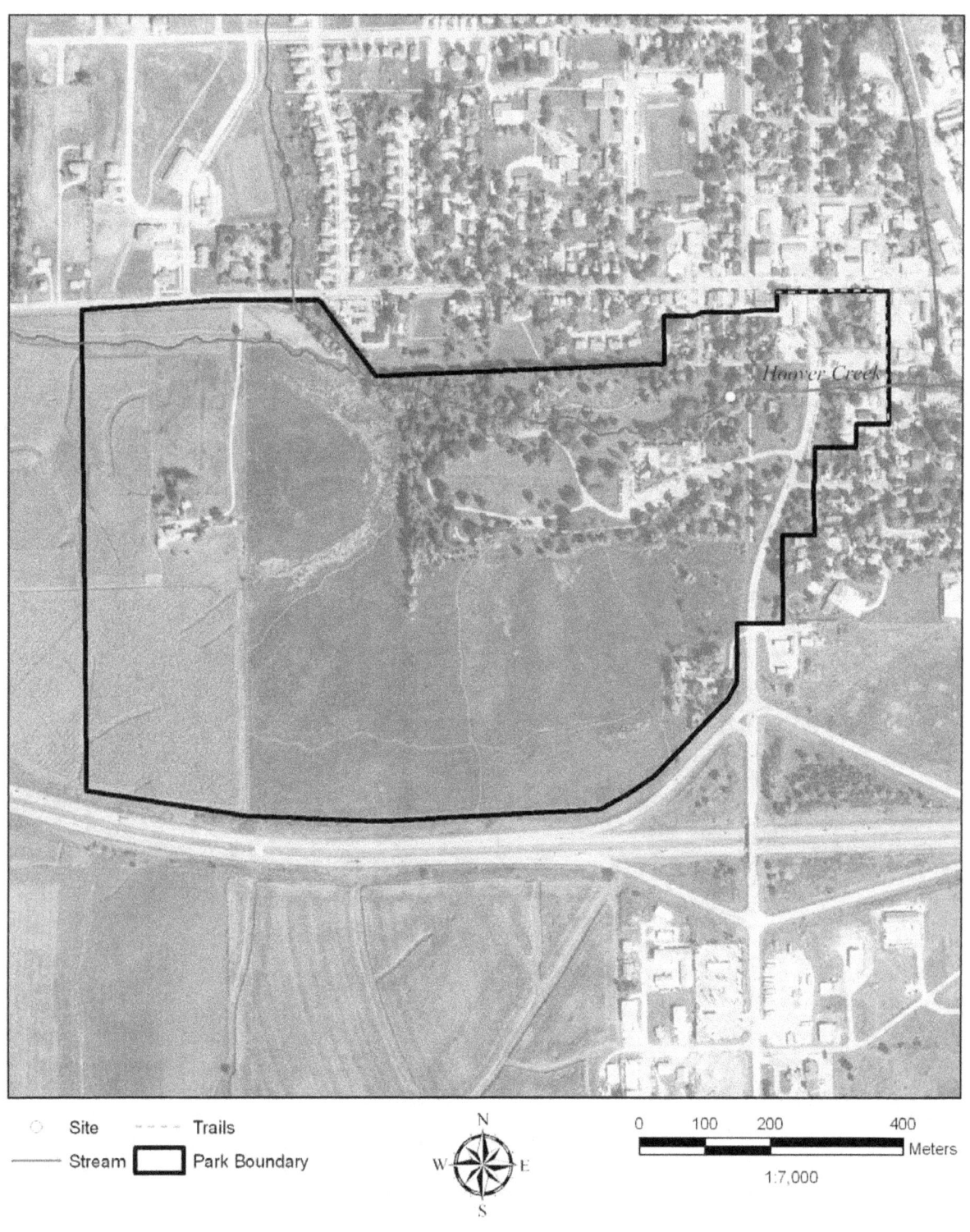

Figure 6. Map of sample site location on Hoover Creek, HEHO.

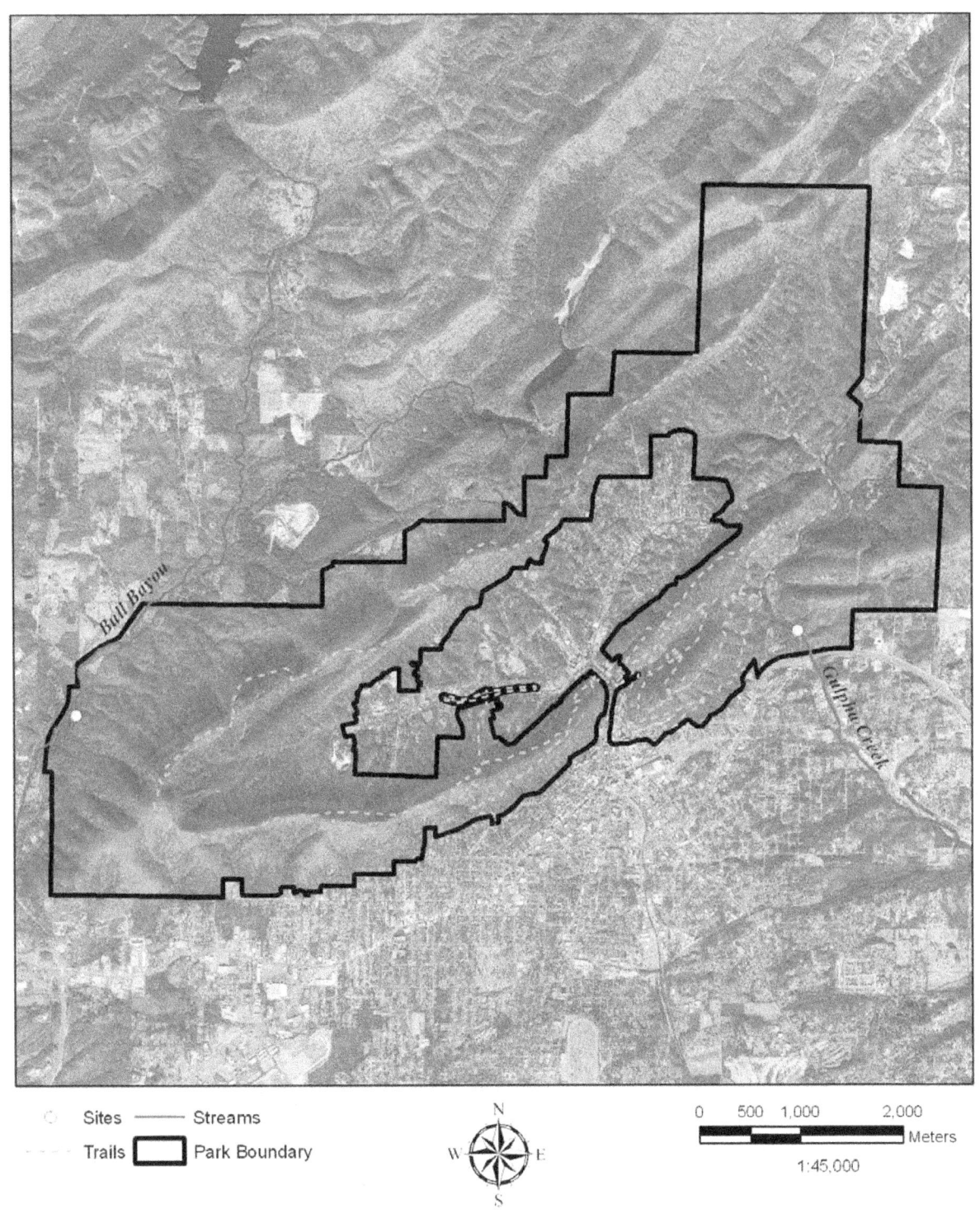

Figure 7. Map of sample sites on Bull Bayou and Gulpha Creek, HOSP.

119

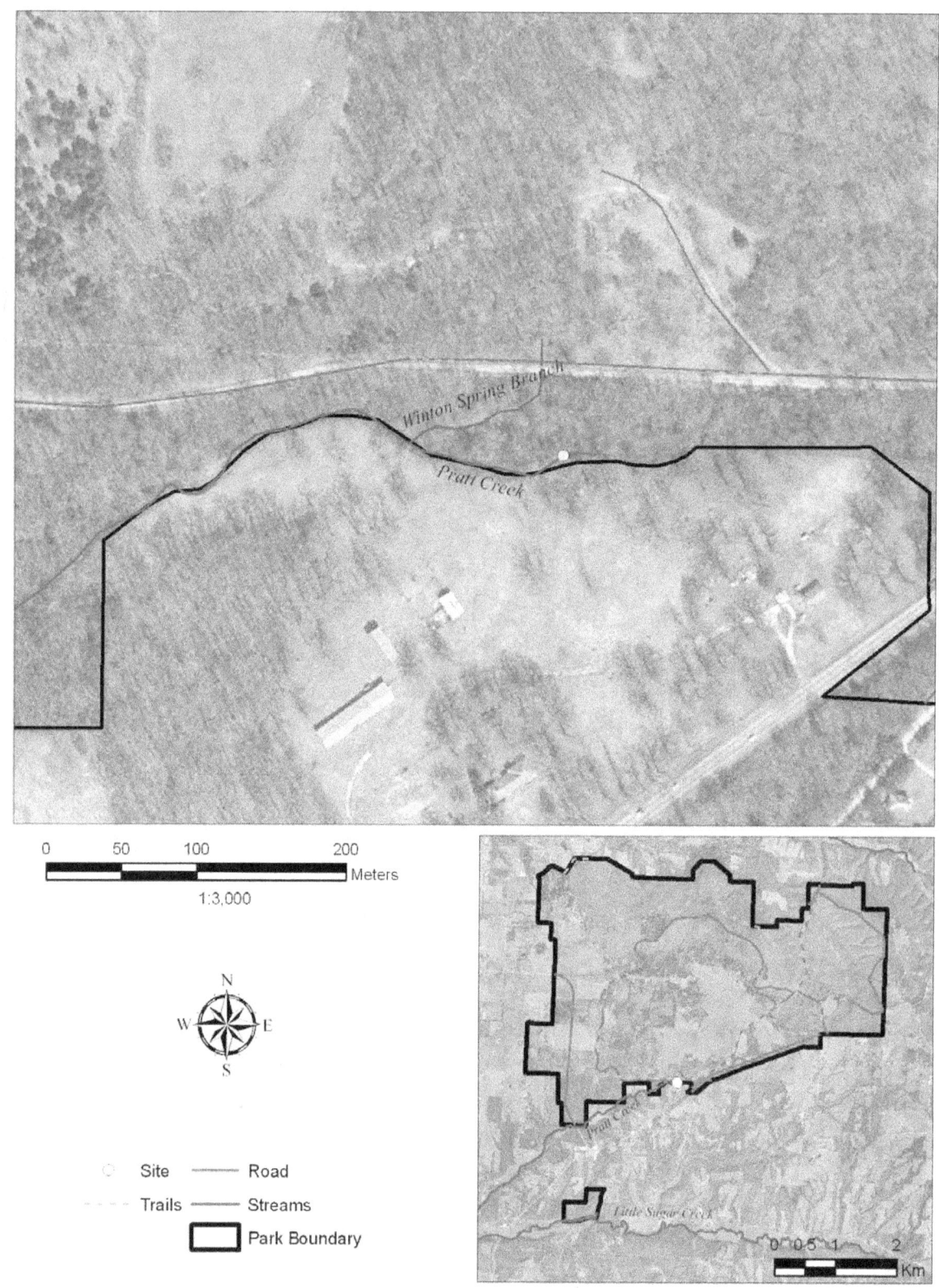

Figure 8. Map of sample site on Pratt Creek, PERI.

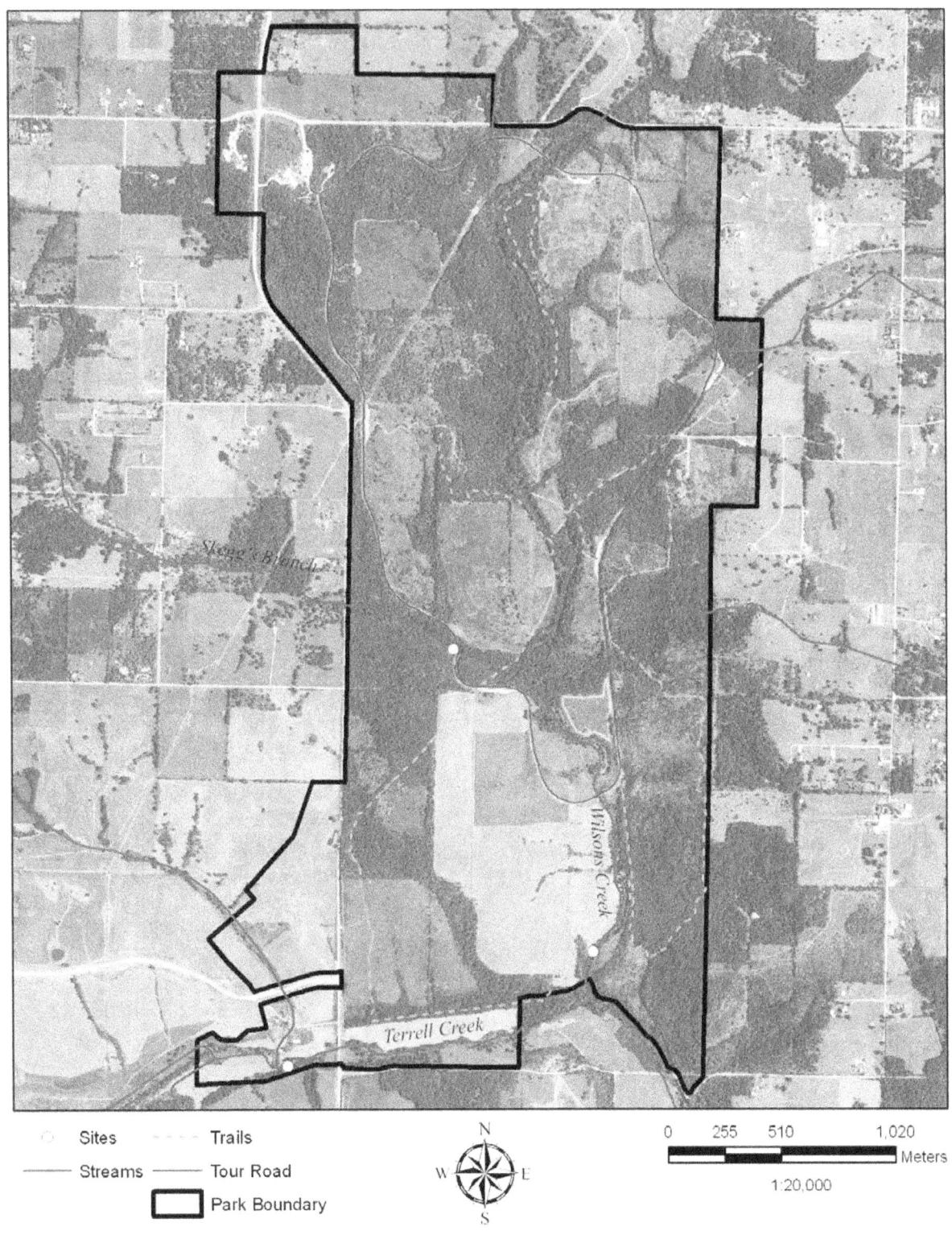

Figure 9. Map of sample sites on Terrell Creek, Skegg's Branch, and Wilson's Creek, WICR.

The NPS has organized its parks with significant natural resources into 32 networks linked by geography and shared natural resource characteristics. HTLN is composed of 15 National Park Service (NPS) units in eight Midwestern states. These parks contain a wide variety of natural and cultural resources including sites focused on commemorating civil war battlefields, Native American heritage, westward expansion, and our U.S. Presidents. The Network is charged with creating inventories of its species and natural features as well as monitoring trends and issues in order to make sound management decisions. Critical inventories help park managers understand the natural resources in their care while monitoring programs help them understand meaningful change in natural systems and to respond accordingly. The Heartland Network helps to link natural and cultural resources by protecting the habitat of our history.

The I&M program bridges the gap between science and management with a third of its efforts aimed at making information accessible. Each network of parks, such as Heartland, has its own multi-disciplinary team of scientists, support personnel, and seasonal field technicians whose system of online databases and reports make information and research results available to all. Greater efficiency is achieved through shared staff and funding as these core groups of professionals augment work done by individual park staff. Through this type of integration and partnership, network parks are able to accomplish more than a single park could on its own.

The mission of the Heartland Network is to collaboratively develop and conduct scientifically credible inventories and long-term monitoring of park "vital signs" and to distribute this information for use by park staff, partners, and the public, thus enhancing understanding that leads to sound decision making in the preservation of natural resources and cultural history held in trust by the National Park Service.

www.nature.nps.gov/im/units/htln/

NPS D-79, August 2008